D.C. Ahir is a reputed scholar of Buddhism, and has made notable contribution to the history of Buddhism. He has to his credit over twenty published books on Buddhism and allied subjects. He retired as Director to the Government of India in 1986, and since then is fully engaged in enriching literature.

GAUTAMA BUDDHA

D. C. Ahir

1994
BOOKS FOR ALL
Delhi-110052

Distributed by
D K Publishers Distributors P Ltd.
24, Ansari Road, Darya Ganj,
New Delhi-110002
Phones: 23201514, 23278368, 23261465
visit us at: www.dkpd.com
e-mail: dkpd@del3.vsnl.net.in

First Published 1994
Reprinted 2003

ISBN 81-7386-257-5

Published by
Books For All
(an imprint of Low Price Publications)
A-6, Nimri Commercial Centre,
Ashok Vihar Phase-IV,
Delhi-110052
Phone: 27401672, 27452453
visit us at: www.lppindia.com
e-mail: lpp@nde.vsnl.net.in

Printed at
D K Fine Art Press P Ltd.
Delhi-110052

PRINTED IN INDIA

CONTENTS

1

A BUDDHA IS BORN

In the sixth century before Christ there was a tiny kingdom in the foothills of the Himalaya, with Kapilavastu as its capital. This kingdom was ruled over by the Sakyas who traced their origin to the great solar race. Their clan name was Gautama. King Suddhodana, the then Sakyan ruler, had married Maya Devi, the beautiful daughter of the neighbouring King of Koliya. In this royal family was born a noble prince who later became a Buddha.

An unusual incident associated with the birth of the Buddha is the wonderful dream which Queen Mahamaya had on the day she conceived. In her dream, she was carried by the guardian angels of the four quarters to the table-land of the Himalaya where she was received by heavenly queens, wives of the four world guardians. Then she was taken to lake Mansarovar (Anotota) where they bathed her, and robed her in divine dress, annointed her with perfumes and decked her with divine flowers. Thence she was taken to the sacred hill nearby on which there was a palace. Here she was laid upon a golden coach facing the east. As she laid her head upon the pillow, she beheld a divinely looking white elephant with six tusks. In its trunk the elephant carried a white lotus. The divine elephant touched her right side and seem to enter her womb.

When Mahamaya related this strange dream to King Suddhodana, he consulted astrologers, who predicted that the Queen would give birth to a son who would be either a universal monarch (Chakravartin) or a Buddha.

On knowing that she was carrying a Great Being in her womb, the pious Mahamaya spent most of her time in prayer and meditation. Then realizing that the time for the birth of her child was coming nearer, Mahamaya sought King's permission to go to her parental home in Davadaha, as was the tradition on such occasions. Mahamaya, seated in a golden palanquin, left Kapilavastu, accompanied by her sister Prajapati and a great retinue. On her way to Davadaha, Mahamaya had to pass through the Lumbini Grove, not far off from Kapilavastu, which was then at its best with numerous flowering trees and trees loaded with fruits. Enchanted by the pleasing sight around, the queen desired to rest for a while, and ordered the couriers to stop. Alighting from her palanquin, she walked up to the foot of a blooming Sal tree. Suddenly she felt the pangs of child-birth. She informed her lady attendants and they put round her a curtain and retired. While she was holding the branch of the Sal tree, the child was born.

While Mahamaya, attended by her sister Prajapati, washed in the nearby tank, the infant to the surprise of all stood up and took seven steps in the Northern direction. At each spot his foot touched, a lotus bloomed.

And there was rejoicing in Heaven and the gods showered flower-petals on him. This sacred day was the Full Moon day in the month of Vaisakha in 623 B.C. or in 563 B.C.

Lumbini, the birth place of the World Honoured Buddha is now in Nepal, just six miles from the Indo-Nepal Border. Asoka, the first Buddhist Emperor, (273-232 BC) had visited Lumbini and worshipped in person the sacred spot where the Buddha was born. An inscription on the Asoka pillar, which stands majestically even today on the site, says: "Twenty years after his coronation, King Priyadarsi, Beloved of the Gods, visited this spot in person and offered worship at this place, because the Buddha, the Sage of the Sakyas, was born here. He caused to be built a stone wall around the place and also erected this stone pillar to commemorate his visit".

Kapilavastu, the capital city of the Sakyas, has since been identified by the archaeologists with Piprahwa, a village in district Basti of Uttar Pradesh. The sacred relics of the Buddha discovered from Kapilavastu (Piprahwa) in 1972 are now preserved in the National Museum, New Delhi. Piprahwa, the site of ancient Kapilavastu, is about fourteen miles from Naugarh, a railway station on the Gorakhpur-Gonda loop line of the North-Eastern Railway, and five miles from Birdpur on the road to Lumbini from Naugarh.

When Mahamaya returned with the child to Kapilavastu, there was great rejoicing in the capital at the good news of the birth of an heir to the King. Now at that time, there lived a great saint, Asita, in a grove not far off from Lumbini. He saw a limitless super radiance in the sky, and was perplexed. On knowing that a Great Being is born in the palace, the sage immediately left for Kapilavastu. Having reached the palace-gates, Asita approached the door-keeper and said, "Go, and tell the king that a sage is waiting at the palace-gate." On being so informed, the King invited the sage into his chamber; offered him a seat and reverently asked the sage the purpose of his visit to the palace. Asita explained the purpose of his visit and wished to see the newly born son of the King. Accordingly, the babe was brought before the sage. Taking the child in his arms, Asita surveyed the auspicious signs on the body of the child, and then contemplated his own future. His eyes welled up, tears began to flow. Seeing the seer sobbing, the King trembled, and in a choked voice he asked Asita as to why he wept. "There is no danger to the Prince. There will be no misfortune for him", Asita said: "I weep not for him, O king, but I wept for myself. The Prince is not an ordinary one. He is a Great Being, he is the future Buddha born for the weal and happiness of the world. But I am now old, aged and advanced in years. As I will not live long and will not be able to listen to his teaching, I am distressed, dejected and unhappy." Then turning to Nalaka, his nephew who was with him, Asita said, "When you hear, Nalaka, that the child has become a Buddha, then go and take refuge in his teachings. This shall be for your weal and welfare and happiness."

On the fifth day, a great name-giving ceremony was held and the child was named Siddhartha, which means "one who has accomplished his aim". Not very pleased with the prophecy of sage Asita, King Suddhodana also wanted the Brahmin soothsayers to see the child and prophecy his future. Of the eight learned Brahmins present on the occasion, seven raised two fingers, and prophesied that either he would become the greatest monarch on earth or he would renounce the world and become a religious leader. However, the youngest of them all, known as Kondanna, raised only one finger, and declared, "There is no reason for this person to remain a house-holder. Stung by the woes of men, he will definitely renounce the world and become a Buddha, an Enlightened One, and unravel the truth to the world".

In the midst of rejoicing over the birth of Siddhartha, Queen Mahamaya suddenly fell ill on the seventh day. Realizing that her end was near, she called Prajapati, her younger sister, who was also married to king Suddhodana, to her bedside, and said, "To you Prajapati, I entrust my child, be thou, a mother to him". On hearing this, Prajapati wept, and promised. Soon thereafter Mahamaya left for her heavenly abode, leaving the child to the care of Prajapati.

Siddhartha was brought up with love and affection by his foster-mother, Mahaprajapati. He was of calm and quiet nature, and loved solitude. At the age of seven, he started his education under the best of the teachers in Kapilavastu. He excelled all other students in study but took no interest in games. One day, with his comrades, he went to see the ploughing festival, which was accompanied by a ploughing match also. He was distressed to see the various insects coming forth from the ground as a result of ploughing, and flocks of birds coming down and devouring them. Seeing the dying insects, his heart was filled with grief. In a reflective mood, he wandered away alone to a lonely place, and sat down under a shady tree. When the King did not see the Prince for a long time, he was filled with anxiety and went in person to seek him in the nearby forest. He found the Bodhisatta[1] there seated cross-legged under a shady tree. He also saw that whereas the shadows of the other trees had turned, the shadow of that particular tree had remained firm giving shelter to the Prince.

Since Siddhartha belonged to a royal (warrior) class, he was taught archery and the use of weapons. But he despised hunting as he did not like causing injury to any living being. Once he showed immense compassion. While he was resting under a tree in his father's farm, a bird fell from the sky in front of him. The bird had been shot by an arrow and was in great agony. He rushed to the help of the bird; he picked up the swan; removed the arrow; dressed the wound and gave it water to drink. In the meanwhile, Devadatta, his cousin, came rushing, and demanded that the bird be handed over to him since he had shot it. Siddhartha refused to do so, saying that it is only he who protects that has right to claim ownership, and not the one who tries to kill. As the dispute persisted, the matter was referred to an arbitrator. The arbitrator upheld the view of the Bodhisatta.

Such were the early traits of the future Buddha.

---

1. A Bodhisatta or Bodhisattva is a person who is destined to become a Buddha. Hence, he is the future Buddha.

2

RENUNCIATION

As the Prince grew up, King Suddhodana, became more worried about the prophecy about his renunciation. He thought of keeping the Prince absorbed in the life of beauty and pleasure. As a first step, he was married to a charming girl Yashodhra. And to make sure that he was fully entangled in the sensual life, the King built three luxurious palaces, one for summer, one for the rainy season and one for winter, equipped with all the requirements and excitements for a full amorous life. He also provided a harem for the prince with beautiful damsels. In this way, he was immersed for nearly ten years in a round of music, dancing and pleasure. Inspite of this life of luxury and beauty, the Bodhisatta was slowly and slowly becoming weary of his surroundings. He felt suffocated in the palace. So, one day, when he was twenty-nine he asked his charioteer, Channa to take him to the city park. On knowing his intention, King Suddhodana ordered that nothing that would make the Prince unhappy and sad should be seen by him, and removed all the unpleasant sights from the roads where the Prince was going to pass. As he rode through the streets of the city, the people of Kapilavastu came out to see the Prince going on special outing. A Sakya maiden Kisagotami saw the Prince from her balcony and filled with joy and delight, she exclaimed: "Happy is the mother, happy is the father, happy is the wife who has such a husband". The future Buddha was also pleased with the sight for some time. But as he was destined to see the three woes of men—decay, disease and death, suddenly there came in view, as if planted by the gods, an old man, tottering on his crutches, which he held with his trembling hands. The Prince was taken aback. He asked the charioteer to move on. When they had gone a little further, a sick man drew near to him, ghastly to look upon, suffering from a deadly disease. The Prince found his sight repulsive, and asked the driver to move on quickly. Going a little further, he saw four men carrying a dead body. On seeing this, the future Buddha commanded Channa, "Take me home". He had been stung by the woes of men; his conscience had been pricked. And the hour of renunciation had arrived. The fourth sight of a dignified hermit, which he also saw, would seem to indicate the way out to find the Truth.

Dejected, distressed and sorrowful, he returned to the palace. Lying on the bed, he reflected on the misery and suffering to which man was subjected to. More he thought, more he became restless. As he lay on his coach, he heard a voice, a cry of agony, as if it were from all humanity: "Arise! O Gotama, Arise for the sake of all human beings! Wait no more! Ye must seek a way of salvation." Silently, he resolved to renounce the world that very night.

While he was in such pensive mood, news came

that his beloved wife Yashodhra had given birth to a son. On hearing this, the Prince exclaimed, "Rahula' meaning a fetter is born". Meanwhile, King Suddhodana ordered festivities to be organised for celebrating the happy occasion. The Bodhisatta took part in the festivities to avoid any misgivings. In the evening, a special programme of music and dance was arranged in his apartment. The musicians and dancers tried their best to entertain the Prince but he took no pleasure in dance and music, and fell asleep. Watching the Prince sleeping, the dancers and musicians thought 'Let us stop and rest for he cannot hear while he sleeps.' They dropped their instruments and fell asleep. When about midnight, the Bodhisatta woke up, what he saw in the dim light of burning oil lamp was awful. "The women with their instruments laid aside were fast asleep. Saliva trickled from the mouths of some; some were covered in sweat; some ground their teeth in sleep; some snored; the garments of some were in disarray". When he saw them thus in their dishevelment, he was more than ever disgusted with the life of passion. 'How wretched it all is. How afflicted it all is ?' he cried, and his mind was set even more strongly on renunciation. So prompted, he rose from his bed and went to the door; called his attendant Channa and asked him to get ready his horse for a long journey.

When he had thus sent Channa, he thought 'I will see my son, and he went to the apartment of the princess and opened the bedroom door. A little lamp of scented oil burned in the inner room. The princess was sleeping on a bed thickly strewn with flowers, with her son's head on her arm. The Bodhisatta set one foot on the threshold and stood gazing at them. 'If I move her hand and take up my son I shall awaken the queen,' he thought, 'and then I shall not be able to go. When I am a Buddha I will come back and see my son'.

So with a manly heart he descended from the palace, and mounted Kanthaka, his favourite white steed, kept ready by Channa. Seated on the horseback, with Channa following, he left the city on the midnight of the fullmoon day of July. As if it was a divine will, the good horse suppressed all noise, that might awaken the attendants; he silenced his neighing, as he went forth with steady steps. Even the gods were ready for the auspicious moment. The four guardians of the four directions held hoofs of the horse on palms so that there is no noise, and the city gates opened miraculously of their own to let the future Buddha go. By day break, he had travelled beyond the boundary of the Sakyan kingdom, and crossed the river Anoma. There, he leapt from his horse, took off his royal jewels, and ordered Channa to take back the same to his father. Saying so, he stepped forward into the wilderness of nature. When Kanthaka saw his master renouncing the world, the horse died broken-hearted. Only Channa returned home to tell the story of Siddhartha's great renunciation.

When alone, the Prince turned a home-less wanderer divested himself of the last vestiges of royalty; cut off his long hair with his sword blade, and changed his royal garments for a monk's dress before proceeding further in search of Truth.

The extreme step taken by Siddhartha was a case of an unprecedented renunciation. He renounced the

world, the world that was his—a kin
wife, a loving son—in order to find a, a beautiful
mankind from suffering. He renounced w to save
pleasures not in old age but in the prime o worldly
not in poverty but in plenty. He had taken the fath;
decision to leave his palace-home, the life of luxu
and pleasure, and to seek solution of his mental-unrest
in the homeless life of an ascetic.

3

ENLIGHTENMENT

Leaving behind all his near and dear ones, discarding all comforts of palace-life, the Prince turned mendicant trekked on foot nearly a distance of about 400 miles and reached Rajagaha(modern Rajgir in Bihar), the capital city of King Bimbisara of Magadha. Entering the city gate in the morning, he went from house to house begging for his alms. His charming personality, dignity and splendid beauty caught the imagination of the people. "So charming and well-groomed", they said, "that he does not seem at all like a mendicant". Soon his arrival in the city became a talk of the town, and reached the ears of King Bimbisara who had in the meanwhile come to know of the dramatic renunciation of Siddhartha, the son of his friend King Suddhodana. Curious to find the truth, Bimbisara went out himself to look for the Prince. In the meanwhile the Bodhisatta had begged sufficient food and retired to the foot of the Pandava hill to take the food in his bowl. Hardly he had finished his meal that King Bimbisara reached the Pandava hill, and addressed the Bodhisatta in these words:

"When I consider thy race, beginning with the sun, thy fresh youth, and thy conspicuous beauty, I wonder whence comes this resolve of thine, so out of all harmony with the rest, set wholly on a mendicant's life, not on a kingdom? Thy limbs are worthy of red sandalwood perfumes—they do not deserve the rough contact of red cloth, this hand of thine is fit to protect subjects, it deserves not to hold food given by another. If, therefore, gentle youth, thou desirest not thy paternal kingdom, then in thy generosity, accept forthwith, one half of my kingdom."

The Bodhisatta politely declined the offer so graciously made by the Magadha King. Convinced of his determination to follow the path he had chosen, Bimbisara begged the Bodhisatta to pay his first visit to him as soon as he had attained enlightenment and found the truth. This the Bodhisatta promised to do.

Continuing his search for truth, the Bodhisatta went to the ashram of Alara Kalama, one of the most prominent teachers at that time. Approaching Alara Kalama, the Bodhisatta said, "Sir, I wish to be initiated into your doctrine and discipline". "You are welcome", said Alara Kalama, "My teaching is such that an intelligent man can before long master it by himself and practice it". With this brief introduction, the Bodhisatta started his training under Alara Kalama. Within a short time, he mastered all what he was taught. No wonder, one day, Alara Kalama announced that he had nothing more to teach him. "You are equal to me now. You are like me; and I am like you", he told Gautama. Now let the two of us teach this assembly of disciples". Not satisfied with what he had learnt, the Bodhisatta took leave of Alara Kalama.

He then went to the ashram of Uddaka Ramaputta,

another well-known teacher who was reputed to teach a stage higher than the seven Dhyanas taught by Alara Kalama. There also, the Bodhisatta soon mastered all what the wise Uddaka Ramaputta taught, and asked him the same question which he had asked Alara Kalama. "Is there anything more to be learnt, Sir." Uddaka Ramaputta gave the same reply, "No friend, there is nothing more that I can teach you". He also invited the Bodhisatta to stay at his ashram and help him teach his pupils but the Bodhisatta declined.

Not satisfied with the teachings of Uddaka Ramaputta, the Bodhisatta marched towards the forest of Uruvela, some 40 miles away, to try asceticism. Meanwhile, on knowing that Siddhartha had renounced the world and set out on the spiritual road, the Brahmin Kondanna, who had originally predicted that the prince would one day become a Buddha, an Enlightened One, also set out from Kapilavastu to join him, along with four other seekers of truth, namely, Bhaddiya, Vappa, Mahanama and Assaji. These five Parivrajakas joined the Bodhisatta in the forest of Uruvela, near modern Gaya in Bihar. Together they started practising asceticism. For six years, the Bodhi-satta practised extreme austerities and self-mortification. Not only he tormented and tortured his body, he also lived on very scanty food; sometimes he lived on wild roots and fruits, or on windfalls only. Consequently, his body had been reduced to a mere skelton. Later, the Buddha himself told his pitiable condition at that time in these words:

"My body became extremely lean....The bones of my backbone were bent like a row of spindles. As the beams of an old bamboo shed stick out, so did my ribs stick out. My body was as if a living skelton. When I thought I would touch the skin of my stomach, I actually caught my backbone, and when I thought I would touch my backbone, I took hold of the skin of my stomach, so much did the skin of my stomach cling to my backbone. To give relief to my body I stroked my limbs with my hand. And as I did so, the decayed hairs fell from my body..."

Such was the condition of Gautama at the end of six long painful years of extreme mortification of the self. Then one day he fell unconscious, and was found by a Shepherd who gave him milk and took him into his care. By and by, the Bodhisatta regained strength and beauty which had been destroyed due to excessive austerities. Thus convinced of the futility of the mortification of flesh, he began taking normal food. When he joined his companions, they were horrified to see him taking food. Annoyed with him on partaking of food, his five companions left him. Thus the Buddha-to-be was left alone to pursue his path.

Determined to achieve enlightenment; to know the ultimate truth, the Bodhisattta now concentrated more on meditative practices and less on austerities. At that time there lived in the neighbourhood a woman named Sujata, daughter of the chief of the village Senani. She was expecting a baby and had vowed that if a son was born to her she would make a special food offering to the deity of a nearby banyan tree. Sujata's vow was fulfilled; she was blessed with a son. So she prepared a special rice-pudding (kheer), and sent her maid to the banyan tree to make necessary arrangements. Meanwhile, the Bodhisatta while wandering had come that way and sat down under that banyan tree to meditate. When the maid came, she was astonished to see an illustrious figure sitting under the tree. She rushed back to tell her mistress that the deity himself had appeared to accept the offering. The grateful Sujata excitedly hurried to the banyan tree, and offered to Bodhisatta the specially prepared rice-pudding in a golden bowl. Sujata was so over-whelmed by the personality of the Buddha-to-be that she reverentially saluted him and withdrew, leaving the precious bowl behind.

After taking the food, the future Buddha came to the Neranjara river, and putting the bowl in the water, he said: "If I am to attain enlightenment, may this golden bowl swim upstream; if not, let it go down". The vessel, indeed, began to float against the current, and at last sank.

Fortified with hope and determination, he crossed the river, to choose a site for his great act of meditation. On the way he met a grass cutter called Sotthiya who gave him some 'kusa grass', a soft pliable grass of which mats are made of. Then the Bodhisatta came to the large pipal tree on the right bank of the river Neranjara, now known as Nilajan, spread the grass at the foot of the shady tree, turned to face the East and sat down cross-legged in a meditating posture. While sitting he vowed to himself: "Let my skin, nerves and bones waste away; let all the flesh and blood in my body dry up, but never from this seat will I stir until I have attained Supreme Enlightenment."

With such determination to attain Sambodhi, he

sat there pondering deep and deep into the mysteries of life. And on that fateful day when he was about to attain Buddhahood, the Mara, the celebrated Lord of Evil Thoughts and Evil Passions, swung into action and attempted in various ways to thwart his efforts. First of all, the Evil One, tried to tempt him with sensual pleasures through his daughters but they failed to attract the attention of the Bodhisatta. When the Mara found that the Bodhisatta was determined to pursue his path, he, in frustration, assaulted him with weapons of darkness, thunder and lightning, storms and hurricans, and sent blast after blast of wind at such velocity as to uproot the forest itself. But all this had no effect on the future Buddha. He remained steadfast on his seat. Looking at the bewildered Mara, he stretched his right hand towards the ground, and said: "May this earth be my witness that I will attain enlightenment and put an end to the sorrows of mankind". Then the earth shook; a great noise arose, and there burst in the sky a thunderbolt making a roaring noise which fell in mid-air. Terrified, Mara's army ran helter-skelter. Having failed to recover the throne to which he had laid claim, Mara disappeared discomforted. The gods celebrated the Bodhisatta's victory; so night fell.

Then entering into deeper contemplation, the Bodhisatta during the first watch of that wonderful night acquired the knowledge of his past lives in various planes of existence; in the second watch he acquired the supernormal divine vision; in the third watch he fathomed the law of cause and effect and gained insight into the destruction of mental cankers; and at sunrise he attained Supreme Enlightenment, Omniscience, and became the Buddha, the Awakened One. Thus, at the age of thirty-five, on the fullmoon day of Vaisakha, Siddhartha reached his goal. He became a Buddha, the Enlightened One, the Awakened One. The Buddha later also came to be known as Sammasambuddha- the Perfectly Enlightened One, Bhagava—the Blessed One, Tathagata- the Perfect One, Sugata—the Happy One or the Accomplished One, and Sakyamuni—the Sage of the Sakyas. The tree under which he sat became known as the Bodhi Tree, and the area as Bodh Gaya. The Land of Enlightenment is seven miles from Gaya in Bihar, and there stands on the site the Great Maha Bodhi Temple, the most sacred shrine for the Buddhists. The sacred Bodhi Tree is to the west of the Maha Bodhi Temple, and the spot sitting where the Buddha attained Supreme Enlightenment is now marked by the Vajrasana or the Diamond Throne seen between the Bodhi tree and the Temple.

The Blessed One, after enlightenment, continued to sit at the foot of the Bodhi Tree enjoying the bliss of Nirvana. He spent the second week in walking to and fro near the Bodhi tree. The third week He spent standing nearby gazing at the Bodhi tree, out of gratitude for giving him shelter. He spent the fourth week in meditation near the Bodhi tree. He spent the fifth week under the Ajapala Nigrodha tree where Sujata had offered him a meal of rice-pudding. He spent the sixth week near the Muchilinda lake where Muchilinda, the Naga King of the lake, is said to have sheltered the Buddha from rain. The Buddha spent the seventh week at the foot of the Rajyatana tree. Here He was offered cakes of barley and honey as food by two merchants, Tapassu and Bhalika, from Utkala, modern

Orissa, who per chance had come there in the course of their travelling.

From the Rajyatana tree, the Buddha returned to the Bodhi tree. Then He thought of making known the New Knowledge which He had gained. He was in two minds, whether to do so or not. He hesitated a bit as He thought that the Dhamma discovered by Him was profound, luminous, subtle, difficult of comprehension, and that the people may not understand it. But soon He was seized with a great pity for the multitude plunged in misery, and with a heart full of compassion the Blessed One decided to disseminate the spiritual illumination for the benefit of all.

4

THE FIRST SERMON

Having enjoyed the bliss of emancipation for seven weeks, the Buddha decided to preach His doctrine, and asked himself, "to whom shall I first teach the doctrine?" The name of Alara Kalama first of all came to His mind. In this way, He thought He will repay His debt to His first teacher. But later, His intution told Him that Alara Kalama was dead. Then He thought of preaching His doctrine to His second teacher, Uddaka Ramputta. But he too was dead. Then He thought that it would be good if this marvellous Dhamma was first of all made known to the five monks who were with Him for a long period of six years in the Uruvela forest, and had left Him in anger due to some misunderstanding on His partaking of food. With these kind thoughts, the Blessed One got up, gazed with reverence at the sacred Bodhi Tree, and thoughtfully proceeded on foot to the deer park about 150 miles away in Isipatana (Rishipatana), modern Sarnath, near Varanasi in Uttar Pradesh, and reached the place in due course where they were staying.

On seeing Gautama coming towards them, the five ascetics decided not to welcome him saying that 'by abandoning austerities and turning to a life of luxury Gautama has committed a sin and is not worthy of respect'.

But when the Buddha came near, all the five Parivrajakas involuntarily rose from their seats and greeted Him. Impressed by His dignified manners and His personality, they treated Him like a distinguished guest.

Still they called Him by His name and addressed Him as "friend Gotama". To put their minds on the right track, the Buddha said : "O monks, Do not call the Tathagata by His name nor address Him as 'friend', for He is the Buddha, the Holy One. Listen to me. I have attained enlightenment, and found a way which can lead one and all to emancipation".

On hearing this, the five Parivrajakas became anxious to hear the Buddha, and requested Him to let them know the new path discovered by Him.

The Middle Path

Responding to their request, the Buddha said:

"There are two extremes, O monks, which he who leads a religious life must avoid. What are these two extremes? One is a life of pleasure, devoted to desire and enjoyment; which is base, ignoble, unspiritual, unworthy and unprofitable. The other is a life of self-mortification; which is painful, and equally unworthy and unprofitable."

"Avoiding both these extremes, the Tathagata has discovered a path, the middle path, which enlightens the mind, opens the eye and bestows understanding, which leads to higher wisdom, to full enlightenment, to Nirvana. And what, O monks, is this middle path, which the Tathagata has discovered, which enlightens the mind, opens the eye and bestows understanding, which leads to higher wisdom, to full enlightenment, to Nirvana? It is the Noble Eightfold Path or the Middle Path, (Majjhima Patipada) as it is called:

Right Understanding	-	Samma Ditthi
Right Thought	-	Samma Sankappa
Right Speech	-	Samma Vaca
Right Action	-	Samma Kammanta
Right Livelihood	-	Samma Ajiva
Right Effort	-	Samma Vayama
Right Mindfulness	-	Samma Sati
Right Concentration	-	Samma Samadhi.

The Four Noble Truths

Continuing the discourse, the Buddha said:

"This, O monks, is the first Truth of Dukkha, Suffering: Life is suffering because of inherent disease, decay and death; meeting with the unliked persons is suffering, parting from those who are liked is suffering; not to get what one desires is suffering. In short, the five aggregates of grasping are suffering.

"This, O monks, is the second Truth of the Cause of Suffering: it is the craving for being that leads from birth to birth, desire for sensual pleasures, desire to have what is not there.

"This, O monks, is the third Truth of the Cessation of Suffering: the way to end suffering is to annihilate desire, give up desire, eliminate desire, tanha, trishna.

This, O monks, is the fourth Truth of the Path that leads to the Cessation of Suffering: it is this Noble Eightfold Path, to wit, Right Understanding, Right Thought, Right Speech, Right Conduct, Right Livelihood, Right Effort, Right Mindfulness, Right Concentration".

Then the Blessed One explained how He had thought, realized, and developed the Four Noble Truths, and how in each case there arose in Him the Vision, Knowledge, Insight, Wisdom, Light, concerning things hitherto unknown.

Finally, He said:

"When I had obtained a clear and proper Vision, Knowledge and Insight regarding these Four Noble Truths, in three phases and twelve ways, then I knew that I had realized perfect and supreme enlightenment. And then, this knowledge and vision arose in me that emancipation of my mind is unshakable; this is my last birth; and there will be no birth again."

The Noble Eightfold Path

The Buddha further said:

1. Right Understanding means to see things as they really are—the true knowledge of suffering, its cause, its cessation and the path leading to its cessation.
2. Right Thought means a pure mind free from lust, free from ill-will and free from cruelty; one's aims, aspirations and ambitions should be noble and praiseworthy, and not ignoble and unworthy.
3. Right Speech means that one's speech should be pure and wholesome; one should abstain from lying,

from slandering, from abusing, from idle talk, and that one should speak kindly and courteously to others.

4. Right Action means that one's deeds should be pure; one should abstain from killing any living creature, abstain from stealing, abstain from sexual misconduct, abstain from false speech, abstain from intoxicants, and thus lead a clean life.
5. Right Livelihood means a mode of living and earning a livelihood through right means; wrong means are trading in arms, in living beings, in flesh, in intoxicating drinks, and in poison; to practise deceit, treachery, soothsaying, trickery, usury is wrong livelihood.
6. Right Effort means effort to avoid evil and unwholesome things and urges; to overcome evil and unwholesome things and urges that have arisen; to develop good and wholesome things and urges; and to maintain good and wholesome things and urges.
7. Right Mindfulness means constant wakefulness of the mind, that is, an alert awareness or contemplation of; all bodily actions or movements, all feelings, all states of consciousness and the objects or contents of the consciousness.
8. Right Concentration means the practice of meditation which leads to a clear understanding of the impermanence of things and ultimately to Nirvana.

Hearing for the first time this exposition of the Four Noble Truths—Suffering; its cause, its cessation; and the path leading to the cessation of suffering—the five Parivrajakas were delighted. At once they realized that this was really a new Dhamma, a new path leading to salvation. Of them, Kondanna was the first to realize the truth. He immediately said, "Venerable Sir, may I become a monk under you and receive ordination."

"Come O monk", pronounced the Buddha,"Well taught is the Dhamma. Lead the noble higher life for the complete extinction of suffering." This was the ordination of Kondanna. Since he was the first to perceive the truth, he came to be called as Annakondanna, 'Kondanna the Wise'. Then his other four companions—Bhaddiya, Vappa, Mahanama and Assaji—one by one, requested the Buddha to accept them as His disciples. "Come O monks", pronounced the Buddha. Thus the Enlightened One gained His first five disciples, and the Wheel of Dhamma began to roll.

The First Sermon of the Buddha at Sarnath, delivered on the fullmoon day of Asadha (July), is known as the Dhammacakka Pavattana' or 'Dharmachakra Pravartana', the Setting in Motion of the Wheel of the Dhamma. The spot where the Buddha first encountered the five Parivrajakas and where He turned the Wheel of the Law is now marked by the Dhamek Stupa, the sole surviving symbol of the ancient glory of Sarnath. As at Lumbini so also at Sarnath, Asoka had erected a monolith pillar in the third century BC. The Lion Capital of the broken Asoka Pillar is now in the Sarnath Museum. The four lions facing the four directions of this capital symbolize the roaring form of the Buddha (Sakyasimha) preaching in all the directions. The Sarnath Lion capital has been adopted as the National Emblem by free India, and the Wheel of the Law (Dharmachakra) now adorns the central part of the National Flag of India.

5

THE WHEEL OF DHAMMA ROLLS ON

The Turning of the Wheel of Dhamma at Sarnath constituted the beginning of the Holy Spiritual and Cultural Empire of Buddhism. Anna Kondanna, Bhaddiya, Vapa, . Mahanama and Assaji, popularly known in the Buddhist Texts as Panchvargiya Bhikkhus, were the first members of the Bhikkhu Sangha established by the Buddha. The sixth person to join the Monastic Order was Yasa or Yasoda. It is said that he was the son of a rich merchant of Varanasi and had all the pleasures and comforts of life to enjoy but he had no liking for all these luxuries. One day he was strolling on the bank of the river Varuna in somewhat dejected mood. Lord Buddha, who was also there, heard him saying 'I am in trouble, I am in distress'. The Blessed One approached him, consoled him and delivered to him relevant discourse which removed Yasa's doubts and he became a Bhikkhu. Meanwhile, Yasa's parents were in great distress on his disappearance, and his father set out in search of him. Towards evening he came across the Buddha, and asked, "Pray, have you seen Yasa, my son". The Buddha said, 'yes', and invited him to come inside. On seeing his son in a monk's robes, "my son, Yasa", said the father, "your mother is very much in grief; she is weeping and wailing; return home and restore her to life". When Yasa said that he would prefer to remain as a Bhikkhu, his father reluctantly reconciled to the changed situation. Before departing, Yasa's father invited the Buddha for meals at his residence. Next day, the Buddha, along with Yasa, went to the house of Yasa's father. After the meals, the Blessed One preached suitably to the family members. Yasa's father, mother and his former wife were delighted, and they became lay disciples of the Buddha.

Now there were four friends of Yasa named Vimala, Subahu, Puranajina and Gawampati, sons of the noble families of Benaras (Varanasi). When they learnt that Yasa has become a disciple of the Buddha, they thought 'what is good for Yasa must be good for them', and joined the Bhikkhu Sangha. Then another fifty of their friends followed their example and became Buddha's disciples, thus making a total of sixty monks within a period of three months.

Encouraged by the response to His doctrine, the Buddha decided to go out on the great missionary campaign. Therefore, on the fullmoon day of October, the Blessed One exhorted His first sixty disciples in these memorable words:

"Go ye, O Bhikkhus, and wander forth for the gain of the many, for the welfare of the many, in compassion for the world, for the good, for the gain, for the welfare of the gods and men. Proclaim O Bhikkhus, the Doctrine Glorious, preach ye a life of holiness, perfect and pure".

Since they were still few in number, and the field to be covered was vast, the Buddha further advised His first batch of missionary monks, saying: "Let not two of you go by the same way".

The Buddha Himself traced His steps back to Uruvela (Gaya). In the course of this journey, He sat down in a grove to rest; and it so happened that there was a party of thirty young men in the same grove enjoying themselves. While they were busy in sports, and no one was paying attention, some of their goods were stolen by a woman. When the theft came to notice, the whole party launched search for the woman, and in the course of the search came upon the Buddha sitting under a tree. Saluting him, one of them said, "Pray, Lord, have you seen a woman pass by with our goods?" The Buddha replied: "which do you think is better; to try and find a woman or to discover yourselves?" Taken aback by this reply, the young men first remained silent; then they cried: "To discover ourselves!". Thereupon, they sat down, and the Buddha preached His doctrine to them.

At that time, there lived in Uruvela a sect of fire worshippers known as Jatilas, matted hair ascetics. This sect was led by three brothers known as Uruvela Kassapa, Nadi Kassapa (Kassapa of the River), and Gaya Kassapa (Kassapa of Gaya). Uruvela Kassapa was the elder and most prominent Kassapa. He had a following of 500 ascetics, and the other two brothers had a following of 300 and 200 ascetics respectively. On reaching Uruvela, the Buddha thought of converting the chief Kassapa, who was also famous for his magical powers.

Reaching his ashram, the Buddha sought Uruvela Kassapa's permission to stay for the night in his place. The Blessed One was offered the room of sacred fire wherein was the fire serpent. The serpent tried to kill the Buddha but all its attempts failed. When the Jatilas came next morning to see the Buddha, whom they thought might have been killed, they were surprised to see the fire serpent tamed and circling round the Buddha. Seeing the Buddha's power and hearing the Buddha's doctrine, Kassapa and other Jatilas threw into the river their things used for fire worshipping and became Buddha's disciples. When the two brothers of Kassapa saw the articles of the Jatilas floating down the river, they came to see as to what had happened. On seeing their elder brother and all his followers dressed as hermits, they were non-plussed and they enquired into the reasons. On being told by Uruvela Kassapa the story of his conversion to the Buddha's Dhamma, Nadi Kassapa and Gaya Kassapa also decided to follow suit, and joined the Sangha.

Accompanied by these new disciples, Lord Buddha proceeded to Rajagriha, Rajgir, the capital of King Bimbisara of Magadha, to fulfil His promise to the king. On knowing that the Sakyan Prince whom he had met years ago and tried in vain to dissuade him from the path of holiness has since become a Buddha, King Bimbisara hastened to visit the Blessed One. The King and other people were astonished to see Uruvela Kassapa, the renowned teacher of the Jatilas, with the Buddha. To dispel their doubts, the Buddha addressed Uruvela Kassapa: "O monk from Uruvela, what made you give up sacrifices".

Kassapa replied: "I gave up faith in sacrifices and offerings as I realized that these things are impure and not leading to the peace of mind and higher wisdom. Hence abandoning sacrifices and offerings aimed at procuring sights, sounds, tastes and other enjoyments, I have gone in quest of the highest Nirvana."

Saying this, the venerable Kassapa got up from his seat, prostrated at the feet of the Buddha, and said:

"O Lord, the Blessed One, you are my teacher, and I am your pupil."

The Buddha then gave a discourse to the King and other elite assembled there. Thereafter, King Bimbisara asked to be accepted as a lay disciple of the Buddha. The King also invited the Buddha and His monks to the palace where he personally served them food. After the meals, Bimbisara presented his pleasure garden, the Bamboo Garden (Veluvana), to the Buddha for the use of the Sangha. The Bamboo Grove monastery later became one of the most important centres of missionary activities of the Buddha. Whenever in Rajgir, He invariably stayed in this monastery.

There resided at that time at Rajgir a religious teacher, Sanjaya, with over 250 disciples. Among them were two young disciples, namely, Sariputta and Moggallana. They were of the same age and were great friends. Both came from the orthodox Brahmin families of the villages Upatissa and Kolita respectively, not far off from Rajgir. They had joined Sanjaya's ashram together. Not satisfied with the teachings of Sanjaya, they were in search of something better, and had agreed among them that whoever first realizes emancipation should inform the other about it.

One day, per chance Sariputta saw Assaji, one of the first five disciples of the Buddha going for alms in the city of Rajgir. Impressed by the dignified and pleasant deportment of Assaji, Sariputta approached him and asked; "Friend, who is your teacher? Whose Dhamma do you profess?"

Assaji replied: "There is, O friend, a great monk of the Sakya clan; that great monk, the Buddha is my teacher; and it is Dhamma of this Blessed One that I follow".

"What is the doctrine of your teacher? What does he preach?", asked Sariputta.

"I am only a novice, my friend", said Assaji. "I came to know this Dhamma and discipline only recently, I cannot explain the Dhamma to you in detail; but I will tell you in short what it means".

"So be it, friend, tell as much or as little as you like, but tell me the essence of it", said Sariputta.

Then the venerable Assaji or Ashvajit recited this Stanza:

"Of all those things that from a cause arise,
Tathagata the cause thereof has told;
And how they cease to be, that too he tells,
This is the doctrine of the Great Sage."

Upon hearing this, Sariputta obtained the pure and spotless eye of truth, and perceived clearly the doctrine, 'whatever is subject to origination is also subject to cessation. "This will suffice", he told Assaji, and asked "where does your teacher live ?"

"He is in this city now in the Bamboo Grove", Assaji said.

On knowing about the Buddha and His teachings in brief from the venerable Assaji, Sariputta rushed back to Sanjaya's ashram, and told all about them to his friend, Moggallana. Soon thereafter, both of them were on their way to the Bamboo Grove monastery.

There the Buddha, seated among the fourfold assembly, was preaching the Dhamma. On seeing them coming from a distance, the Blessed One said, "There come the two friends who will be two excellent disciples to me, a blessed pair."

Having reached where the Buddha was sitting, the two seekers of truth saluted the Buddha reverently, and sat down on one side. Then, with folded hands, they said, "May we join, O Lord, the Sangha of the Blessed One; may we obtain the ordination". The Buddha said: "Come, O Bhikkhus! Well preached is the Dhamma. Now live the life of Purity, to attain the highest Nirvana", this was their ordination. Shortly afterwards, both of them attained sanctification, and became masters of the Dhamma. Later, the Buddha bestowed upon Sariputta and Moggallana the rank of Chief Disciples.

After Sariputta and Moggallana had left Sanjaya, there was a revolt in Sanjaya's ashram. And all his disciples deserted Sanjaya, and sought refuge in the Buddha-Dhamma.

From Rajgir, the Buddha went for a time to Sarnath where He spent the first Vassa, Retreat during the rainy season. He then came back to Rajgir via Uruvela.

In the meanwhile, His father Suddhodana sent envoy after envoy to invite then Buddha to Kapilavastu. But all failed to convey the message. Then King Suddhodana sent Kaludayi, his chief minister, to invite the Buddha to Kapilavastu. On getting the message, the Buddha promised to visit Kapilavastu after sometime. When the Buddha, accompanied by Sariputta, Moggallana and other monks, arrived in Kapilavastu, He stopped at the Banyan (Nyagrodha) Grove outside the city, where He was first of all worshipped by His father and other kinsmen. Next day, the Buddha accompanied by His disciples, entered the city for alms and went from house to house. When this came to the notice of King Suddhodana, he felt ashamed, and rushed to the place where the Buddha was begging. The King remonstrated the Buddha saying that such conduct was unworthy of his race. "Yours, O King is the lineage of Kings, but mine is that of the Buddhas, who have always begged for food", replied the Buddha. Later, agreeing to the request of the King, the Buddha and His disciples went to the palace where they were served the best of food. After the meal, all the ladies of the palace came to pay respect to the Buddha, excepting his wife, Yasodhara. Then, accompanied by Sariputta, the Blessed One Himself went to the apartment of Yasodhara. There she held the feet of the Buddha and worshipped Him.

During Buddha's first visit to Kapilavastu, atleast two of his kinsmen joined the Sangha, but both in dramatic circumstances. Prince Nanda, the son of Suddhodana by Mahaprajapati, and step-brother of the Buddha, was the first Sakyan prince to join the Sangha. He was now thirty-five, the aging King Suddhodana appointed him as the Crown Prince, in place of Siddhartha, and also arranged his marriage with a princess, one Janapada Kalyani. He combined these festivities with the Buddha's visit to the Sakyan capital. The wedding of Nanda and Janapada Kalyani took place on the third day after the Buddha's arrival, and the Buddha duly attended. After the wedding, He blessed the couple and then the rest of the gathering departed. When the Buddha got up to depart, He gave his bowl to Nanda. Thinking that this was momentary, Nanda said nothing. But soon the Buddha left the place without saying anything. Nanda followed behind Him, and ultimately reached the monastery. When Nanda handed back the bowl to the Buddha, he met with a surprise. Instead of thanking him, the Buddha bluntly asked Nanda if he would like to join the Sangha. Dazed Nanda, did not know what to say. He had great respect for the Buddha, who was also his elder brother. Hence, he could not say no, and reluctantly agreed to join the Order. Soon thereafter, Nanda was ordained by Sariputta, who along with many other monks, had accompanied the Buddha to Kapilavastu.

Since Nanda had joined the Order of wandering monks on his wedding day, he could not adjust easily to the life of an ascetic. He still dreamt of his beautiful abandoned bride, and felt unhappy and homesick. He also still went about in a fashionable way wearing fine clothes. When Nanda's unhappiness was reported by his fellow monks to the Buddha, the latter personally took him in hand. 'Nanda,' He said, 'you are one of my clan who out of faith have forsaken the domestic life for one of homelessness. It is not right that you should wear carefully pressed robes, use cosmetics and carry a bowl of glazed pottery. You should live like other monks'.

The Buddha gradually weaned Nanda away from his worldly concerns, and in particular, his yearning for his wife. And eventually Nanda became an exemplary disciple of the Buddha.

A touching scene at Kapilavastu was the ordination of Rahula, Buddha's son, who was born on the day he left home to seek enlightenment. It so happened that on the seventh day of Buddha's stay at Kapilavastu, when the Blessed One was on the round, Yasodhara, his wife, pointing out from the window to Rahula that Buddha was his father, asked him to go and ask for his inheritance. Rahula then went to the Buddha, Buddha blessed him and marched further. But Rahula followed him. Then the Buddha turned to Sariputta, saying: "Give him the inheritance of a holy life, which is the only treasure that I have". So Rahula was admitted to the Sangha when just a child. As ordination of Rahula deprived Suddhodana of all possible male heirs to his kingdom, he complained to the Buddha saying that 'when you left home I was very, very, sad' and when Nanda joined the Sangha I was also very unhappy. Now, you have taken away Rahula, my last hope'. He further said that Rahula being a child should not have been ordained without his consent. Though Rahula stayed as a monk but a rule was made that in future no minor should be admitted to the Sangha without the consent of his parents.

Rahula was just seven years old when he became a monk. Since he was just a child, the Buddha appears to have taken special interest in his training. One episode recorded in the Majjhima Nikaya shows the Buddha teaching Rahula like a loving father.

When Rahula was eleven years old, he was staying in the Ambalathika monastery at Rajgir. The Buddha also came to Rajgir and took up residence in the Bamboo Grove monastery. One evening, the Blessed One, having risen from meditation, went to see Rahula. Seeing the Buddha coming from afar, Rahula got ready a seat, and water for washing the feet. After usual greetings, the Blessed One sat down on the seat prepared for Him. Rahula, having saluted the Buddha, sat on one side.

Thereupon, the Blessed One having poured a small quantity of water into a vessel addressed young Rahula:

"Do you see Rahula, the small quantity of water in the vessel ?"

"Yes, Lord".

"Similarly, Rahula, insignificant is the virtue of those who are not ashamed of telling lies."

Then the Buddha threw away that small quantity of water, and addressed Rahula:

"Do you see, Rahula, that quantity of water I threw away ?"

"Yes, Lord".

"Similarly, Rahula thrown away like this is the virtue of those who are not ashamed of telling lies."

Then the Blessed One turned the water-vessel upside down, and addressed Rahula:

"Do you notice, Rahula, this vessel turned upside down?"

"Yes, Lord".

"Similarly, Rahula, overturned indeed is the virtue of those who are not ashamed of telling lies."

Finally, the Blessed One turned the water-vessel upright, and addressed Rahula :

"Do you see, Rahula, this water-vessel now quite empty ?"

"Yes, Lord" ?

"Similarly, Rahula, empty and void is the virtue of those who are not ashamed of telling lies".

"So Rahula, you must train yourself never to speak untruth even jokingly".

Concluding the lesson, the Buddha asked: "what do you think a mirror is for, Rahula?"

"To look at one self, Lord," replied Rahula.

"Right", said the Buddha. " In the same way, Rahula, you should always keep on looking, reflecting at your acts of body, of speech and of mind."

From Kapilavastu, the Buddha returned to Rajgir. About the same time, Sudatta, a wealthy merchant of Sravasti or Savatthi, who because of his exemplary charity to the poor was popularly known as Anathapindika, meaning 'the feeder of destitute', happened to visit his sister who was married to a rich merchant of Rajgir. On arriving there, he found to his astonishment that his brother-in-law hardly noticed him. He was very busy eagerly making elaborate preparations for meals for a large number of people. On knowing that Lord

Buddha and his monks had been invited for a meal the following day, Anathapindika became attentive. "Did you say the Buddha, the Enlightened One ?", he asked, 'Indeed', answered his brother-in-law, "tomorrow the Blessed One is coming." On hearing this, Anathapindika became eager to meet the Buddha. Moved by many kinds of thoughts, he could not even sleep properly. Early next morning he set out to meet the Buddha, who was staying in the monastery on the outskirts of the city. Approaching the monastery, he saw in the misty dawn a figure walking silently to and fro. Anathapindika stopped. Then the figure called to him in a very sweet voice: "Come, Sudatta!"

Anathapindika was amazed at being addressed in this manner, for no one there knew him by his original name. He was only known as Anathapindika, and besides, he was unknown to the Buddha and had come unexpectedly. Now he was certain that he was in the presence of the Enlightened One. Overwhelmed by this encounter, he fell at the feet of the Buddha, and asked Him in a stammering voice the convential question about His well-being. "The Arahats are always well", the Buddha said, "for they are beyond all possibilities of suffering". And then the Blessed One, leading him step by step, explained to Anathapindika the essence of the noble eightfold path. With that, the pure eye of truth opened for Anathapindika. Having understood the truth of the Teaching , he was without any wavering, certain in his mind, he took refuge in the Buddha-Dhamma, and invited the Blessed One to visit Sravasti his home town in Kosala. The Buddha promised to visit Sravasti soon.

On returning to Sravasti, Anathapindika decided

to build a suitable monastery for the reception of the Buddha. The only suitable site that could be found near Sravasti was the park of Prince Jeta, son of King Prasenajit, Pasenadi. When Anathapindika asked the prince to sell the park, Jeta demanded an exhorbitant price, viz., 'as many gold pieces as will cover it". Anathapindika at once agreed, and proceeded to cover the ground with gold coins from his treasury. As the gold they brought at first was not enough to cover the whole ground and there was a small space near the gate that was left uncovered, Anathapindika ordered his men to go and fetch more gold to cover that space. Then it occurred to Prince Jeta: 'this can be no ordinary matter since Anathapindika is spending so much gold'. He asked Ananda to desist; not to cover that space. "Leave me that space. It shall be my gift", he said. In deference to the wishes of the Prince Jeta, Anathapindika left that space uncovered. Later, on the uncovered ground Jeta himself erected a gate. Anathapindika also spent a huge amount to raise the magnificent Vihara, and other shrines and monasteries. It is said that the dedication of the Vihara was ceremonially gone through in the presence of the Buddha. And the Buddha, in order to commemorate the pious gifts of both, ordered that the Vihara should be called" Anathapindika-arama of Jetavana-Vihara".

Having built a vast monastic complex, Anathapindika also assumed responsibility for its upkeep and proper maintenance. He supplied the monks who lived there with all necessities. Not only he sent each morning meals to the monastery but he also took care of all the requirements of clothing, almbowls and medicines. And several hundred monks came daily to his home a seven storey palace—to receive the noon meal. Having regard to these facilities and Anathapindika's devotion, Jetavana in due course, became almost a regular residence for the Buddha. It was the practice of the Blessed One to be on the move for eight months in a year, and spend the four month Vassa, Retreat during the rainy season, at one place. Of the forty-five such Retreats, the Buddha spent as many as nineteen Vassa periods in the Jetavana monastery.

Whenever the Buddha stayed in the Jetavana, Anathapindika would usually visit Him twice a day just to have darshan of the Blessed One, but frequently to hear a discourse. Occasionally, he would ask questions also to have his doubts cleared. A number of instructions to Anathapindika given by the Buddha have been recorded in the Pali Canon.

The Buddha spent the fifth Retreat at the Kutagara hall of the Mahavana grove in Vaisali. From there, He again went to Kapilavastu on knowing that there was an imminent danger of war between the Sakyas and the Koliyas on the question of distribution of the waters of the Rohini river in a season of drought. When the two armies, which were almost face to face, saw the Buddha coming, they put down their weapons, and worshipped the Blessed One.

"What is fight, great Kings?" asked the Buddha.

When He was told that it was a quarrel over water, the Buddha asked: "which do you think, O kings, more valuable? The lives of the kings, nobles and other men or the water."

"The human lives, O Lord, are more valuable", they answered.

Then the Buddha asked: "Is it proper for you to destroy invaluable human lives for the sake of water of little value?"

Realizing their folly, the Sakya and Koliya armies lowered their war standards, and made peace.

After the war threat was over, the Sakyan princes resolved to join the fraternity of the monks. One day six Sakyan princes together with Upali, the court barber, and an armed escort, set out from their homes intending to join the Sangha. The six princes were: Bhaddiya, Anuruddha, Ananda, Bhagu, Kimbila and Devadatta. To avoid suspicion over the purpose of their departure, they left as if on their usual outing to the pleasure garden. Having gone a little far from the city, they sent the escort back. After going a little further they took off their ornaments, and gave them to Upali, saying, "This will be enough for your life-time. Now return home!" After taking a few steps back, Upali stopped, and thought: "If the princes can discard this wealth, why should I cling to it. It is better I join them." So he hung the bundle of ornaments on a tree, and rushed back to join the princes. He told them what he had done, and said: "If you, O Princes, are going forth into the homeless life of monkhood, I would also do the same?"

The Sakyan princes were moved, and allowed Upali to join them on their way to see the Blessed One. Having arrived where the Buddha was staying, they asked for ordination. While doing so, Ananda said: "Lord,we Sakyan Princes are proud. Please admit Upali, our barber, first in the Order so that he shall be our Elder and we have to salute him". Pleased with the proposal, the Buddha ordained Upali first of all. In due course, Upali became the foremost monk among the disciplinarians. He was the chief authority for the rules of discipline (Vinaya Pitaka) at the time of the First Buddhist Council held at Rajgir after the Maha-parinirvana of the Buddha.

Of the six Sakyan princes, Anuruddha, Ananda and Devadatta, in particular, played a significant role in the Bhikkhu Sangha; the first two a positive role and the third, Devadatta a negative role.

Anuruddha and Ananda were the sons of the prince Amitodana, younger brother of King Suddhodana. Anuruddha was the foremost in developing the divine eye, and was a great meditator. His younger brother Ananda is well-known as the personal attendant of the Buddha. He was 37 when Ananda joined the Order. For the first 18 years, he was not much known in the Sangha. Silently, he was fully occupied with the purification of his mind. Then one day when he was 55, and so was the Buddha, the Blessed One called a meeting of the monks and declared: "In my 20 years as a monk, as Founder of the Sangha, I have had many different attendants but none of them has really filled the post perfectly. Now I am 55 years old and it is necessary for me to have a trustworthy and reliable attendant." At once all the chief disciples offered their services. But the Buddha did not accept.

Then the Buddha looked at Ananda, who had held back modestly, thinking that it was for the Blessed One to choose a suitable attendant, and declared that Ananda would be pleasing to him, acceptable to him as his attendant. Ananda thanked the Buddha for reposing so much confidence in him. The Sangha too gladly approved his appointment.

Ananda's devotion to the Buddha was total. For the next 25 years until the Buddha's Parinirvana, he remained attached to the Buddha like a shadow; His constant servant, keeping His room tidy, washing His bowl and robes, doing all other sundry jobs, and always keeping close to the Buddha in case he was needed. The Buddha once described Ananda as a learned, mindful, well-behaved and resolute disciple. So great was Ananda's devotion to the Buddha that he even neglected his own meditation. As a result, he could not attain Arahatship during the life time of the Buddha. Only afterwards he did so.

The third visit of the Buddha to Kapilavastu, His home town, was on learning about the demise of His father, King Suddhodana. A significant incident during this visit was the request by Mahaprajapati, His foster-mother, now widowed, to join the Sangha and follow the royal road to Nirvana. Three times she pleaded for permission to adopt an ascetic's life, and three times, she got the same reply, "Enough O Gotami, do not insist that women should be allowed to do so." This refusal saddened Mahaprajapati, and she went away weeping.

From Kapilavastu, the Buddha returned again to Vaisali to spend His fifth Retreat. Some time after that, Mahaprajapati, His foster-mother, Yasodhara, His former wife, and many other Sakyan ladies, arrived in Vaisali. Covered with dust and with sweat, Mahaprajapati stood outside the Kutagara hall in the Nigrodha Park, sad and sorrowful. Ananda saw Mahaprajapati in that pitiable state and asked as to why she was there. She explained that she was dejected and disappointed as the Buddha had refused to grant ordination to women. Impressed by her zeal and determination, Ananda undertook to plead her case with the Buddha. Taking along Mahaprajapati to the Buddha, Ańanda asked three times, saying, "It were well ? O Lord, if women were given permission to join the Sangha." But it was of no avail, the Buddha remained adamant; silent. Pursuing his argument further, Ananda asked the Blessed One whether the women were not as capable as men of leading a contemplative life and of treading on the path of arhatship. Without any hesitation, the Blessed One said that sex was no bar to the attainment of sainthood, arahatship." So saying, the Buddha agreed to permit ordination of Mahaprajapati, Yasodhara and other Sakyan ladies, subject to certain conditions. Thus a separate Order of Nuns, the Bhikkhuni Sangha came into being five years after the Buddha had launched His missionary campaign. Once the Order of Nuns was established, the women were on equal footing. This ensured an honoured place for women in the society. It is significant that at least 12 of the 80 great disciples of the Buddha were women.

Thus within five years, the Buddha had gained considerable following. For the next forty years, the Blessed One travelled constantly from town to town, village to village, preaching His message of equality; of hope and peace; of kindness and compassion. As small rivulets flow towards the ocean so rushed the recluses, scholars, philosophers and lay folk towards the Buddha. The Buddha did not show any preference for any group or class of people. Irrespective of caste, colour or status, He admitted all into the Sangha who were willing to lead a holy life. He said: "just O brethren, as the great rivers—Ganga, Yamuna, Aciravati, Saraswati and Mahi—when they have fallen into the great ocean, loose their different names and are known as the great ocean—just so, O brethren, do these castes, when they begin to follow the doctrine and discipline as propounded by the Tathagata, they renounce different names of castes and rank, and become members of one and the same society."

As such, disciples of the Buddha, both monks and lay, came from all walks of life. They included rich and poor, high and holy and low and lowly. Some of his eminent disciples came from the so-called lower classes. Not only that, they also enjoyed equal status and privileges, and were given positions of status. For instance, Upali, the barber, was the chief in matters relating to the rules and regulations of the Sangha. And Sunita, the scavenger, was a celebrated figure in the Sangha. The low-born Sunita tells the story of his first encounter with the Blessed One in these words:

"I was born in the low caste, was poor and had very little to eat. I did the low work of a scavenger. Despised and humiliated by the people, I felt frustrated. Then one day I saw the Buddha entering the city of Rajgir in the company of monks. I threw away my baskets and went forth to worship the Buddha, and He stood before me out of compassion. After saluting the Buddha, I stood aside and begged for ordination.The Buddha said: "Come O monk', and that was my ordination."

After this simple ordination, the Buddha took Sunita

to the monastery; invested him with bowl and robes; taught him the Dhamma, and said, "By the discipline of holy life, restraint and mastery of self, a man becomes holy." Sunita later became a celebrated figure in the Sangha, enjoying the respect of all. When asked how Sunita became so great, the Buddha said, "As on a rubbishheap on highway cast a lily may grow, fragrant, and sweet, so among rubbish creatures, worldings blind by insight shines the very Buddha's child."

Among other low-born persons admitted into the Sangha by the Blessed One were: Sopaka, an abandoned child in the cemetery at Sravasti; Suppiya, who performed the duties of watchman in the same cemetery; 'Sumangala, a peasant of Sravasti; Kappata-Kura a rag picker who lived in Sravasti, Dhanniya, a potter of Rajgir, and Suppabuddha, a leper of Rajgir.

Among the low born women who came to the refuge of the Buddha and joined the Sangha, the name of Prakriti shines above all. It so happened that while the venerable Ananda was staying at Sravasti, he went on some mission to a far off place. On his way back, he felt thirsty. As he passed by a village, he saw a girl fetching water from a well. Approaching her he asked her to give him some water to drink. The girl belonged to the lowest rung of untouchables, and said, "Sir, I am of low caste". Ananda replied: "Sister I have not asked your caste, I have asked for water. Please give me some water to drink." Whereupon the Matanga girl joyfully gave Ananda water to drink.

The venerable Ananda thanked her and went away; but Prakriti having taken fancy for Ananda, followed him at a distance. Later, we are told, that her mother tried through magic spell to get Ananda to marry Prakriti. And it was through the intervention of the Buddha that not only Ananda was saved from this embarrassment, but Prakriti was also prompted to join the Sangha as a nun. In due course, Prakriti became a renowned figure in the Sangha.

Some other low-born nuns who attained sanctification were: Punna, a slave girl; Kapa, the daughter of deer-stalker; Subha, the daughter of a smith; and Ambapali, a courtesan. There are many such instances where the Buddha emancipated the depressed and oppressed, sinners and criminals besides kings, queens, nobles and other rich elite.

One of the notable lay disciples of the Buddha was Jivaka, the noted Physician and Surgeon of Rajgir. Jivaka was the son of Salvati, a courtesan of Rajgir. Immediately after birth, the child was placed in a basket and thrown on a dust heap. When the child was discovered, a large crowd gathered there. Abhaya, the Rajkumar of Magadha, also happened to pass that way. He saw the people curiously looking at the dust-heap. On being told that there was a newly born abandoned child, and that it is alive, Abhaya took the child home. He called him Jivaka. When Jivaka grew up, he came to know the circumstances under which he was saved. He, therefore, resolved to qualify himself as a doctor to save others. He went to Takshila, and studied medicine there for seven years. On return, Jivaka set up his practice at Rajgir and became a popular doctor. He was also appointed King Bimbisara's personal Physician. As soon as Jivaka came into contact with the Buddha, he became a lay devotee. The Blessed One did not make him a

Bhikkhu as He wanted Jivaka to remain free to tend to the sick and ailing people.

The first two chief disciples of the Buddha, Sariputta and Moggallana, hailed from the villages near Rajgir (Rajagriha). Another chief disciple who hailed from the same area was Maha Kassapa. His original name was Pipphali Kassapa, and he had inherited a large landed property from his father. He was married to the beautiful Kapilani of Sagala in the Madda country (Punjab). One day, he saw that when his men ploughed, many birds gathered and eagerly picked the worms from the furrows. This sight, so common to a farmer, suddenly startled him, and the killing of worms as a result of ploughing forcefully pricked his conscience. Shaken by this sight, he decided to say good-bye to the worldly life.

Going home, he broached the subject to his wife, Bhadda Kapilani. She had also been thinking somewhat on the same lines. Hence, both decided to take to the life of an ascetic. Putting on ascetic garbs, they left their estate, unnoticed by the servants, in search of the Buddha about whom they had heard. When walking on, Kassapa went ahead and Kapilani followed him. Considering this not appropriate, when they reached at crossroads, Kassapa said: "Bhadda, you take one of these roads, and I shall go the other way." So they parted.

The Buddha perceived that an outstanding disciple was on the way to Him. He then set out on the road to Nalanda Himself. After going a little distance, the Buddha sat down under a fig tree, waiting for His future disciple. When Kassapa arrived there and saw the radiance of Buddha's aura, he thought, "This must be my Master, the Buddha, for whose sake I have gone forth!" He approached the Buddha, fell at His feet and exclaimed: "The Exalted One, Lord, accept me as your disciple!"

The Buddha said, "Come O monk", and asked Kassapa to sit down. He then gave a brief sermon to Kassapa on the virtues of Dhamma. Then, both Master and disciple walked towards Rajgir. On the way, the Buddha wanted to rest and went off the road under the shade of a tree, Kassapa then folded his double-robe four-fold and requested the Buddha to sit on it. The Buddha sat down on Kassapa's robe and said: "Soft is your robe of patched cloth, Kassapa.". Hearing this, Kassapa replied: May the Blessed One, O Lord, accept this robe of patched cloth out of compassion for me". "But, Kassapa, can you wear these rough, worn-out rag-robes of mine?" Full of joy, Kassapa said: "Certainly, Lord, I can wear the Blessed One's rough and worn-out rag-robes."

The exchange of robes by the Buddha with Maha Kassapa is the solitary example of its kind in the whole life of the Buddha. Apparently, He thoughtfully did so to inspire Kassapa to observe the "austere practices", which Kassapa later did, and excelled all others in that. He became a father figure in the Sangha, and it was Maha Kassapa, who, after the Mahaparinirvana of the Buddha, convened the First Buddhist Council at Rajgir, and also presided over it.

Bhadda Kapilani, Maha Kassapa's wife also in due course joined the Sangha and attained Arahatship.

Another prominent disciple of the Buddha who showed a great spirit of self-abnegation was Ratthapala, a Kuru noble. Once the Buddha was on a missionary tour in the Kuru country. He stayed at Thullakotthita, a town of the Kurus, in modern Haryana. When the inhabitants of this town came to know of the arrival of the Blessed One, they came to listen to the Buddha's discourse. Among them was a young man named Ratthapala (Rashtrapal), a scion of a leading family of the place. After the Buddha had finished His discourse and all others had gone, Ratthapala approached the Blessed One and showed his keenness to become a monk. The Buddha asked him to have the permission of his parents before adopting the life of a monk. Ratthapala went home and with great difficulty obtained the permission of his parents to join the Sangha and that too on the condition that, 'he must come and see them occasionally'. Promising to do so, Ratthapala went back to the Buddha and reported that his parents had since given him permission to become a Bhikkhu. Saying so, he sought admission to the fraternity of the monks. Admission was granted. Soon afterwards, the Buddha left for Sravasti. Ratthapala also accompanied.

In a very short time Ratthapala became well-versed with the Dhamma and attained the stage of Arahatship. One day he approached the Buddha and sought permission for paying a visit to his parents. Scanning the thoughts of Ratthapala's heart, and recognizing that he was incapable of abandoning his training and reverting to the life of a layman, the Buddha permitted him to go.

Then rising up and thanking the Lord, Ratthapala set out to visit his parents. Reaching Thullakotthita, he headed towards his father's house. At that time, his father was having his hair-cut. He saw the yellow-robed monk from a distance and started murmuring that these shaven-headed monks have snatched his son from him. And when Ratthapala came near him, he, without looking at him, abused the monk and forced him to return with the empty begging bowl. So, at his father's house, Ratthapala got nothing, but abuse.

On his way back, Ratthapala saw a maid-servant going to throw away some stale rice. He asked the maid-servant, "Sister, if you want to throw away this gruel, kindly put it into my bowl". As she was doing so, she recognised that the mendicant was none else but her master's only son. She rushed back and told Ratthapala's mother that her son has come back, and is just nearby. Overwhelmed by the news, Ratthapala's mother went to her husband, and asked him to go at once and bring their son for the meals.

Meanwhile, Ratthapala had gone out of the town and was taking his meal under the shade of a tree. When his father found him, he said: "Ratthapala dear, why are you eating stale porridge ? "You could have come to your own home."

"Where, householder, is there a home for us who have goneforth from the home-life into homelessness? We are homeless ones. Of course, I did come to your house, householder, but I got neither alms nor polite refusal, only abuse I got."

Then, seeking pardon for the mal-treatment meted out to Ratthapala, his father said: "Come Ratthapala dear, let us go to the house."

"Not so, householder, I have taken my meal for

the day," said Ratthapala. Then, his father requested Ratthapala to take next day's meal with them. Ratthapala agreed.

Next day, at the appointed hour, the venerable Ratthapala, duly robed and with begging bowl in hand, went to his father's house. Since his father wanted to entice him away from the monkish life, he placed a large heap of the family's wealth, gold coins and bullion, and pleaded with him 'to abandon his training and revert to the life of the layman', saying that if he will not revert to lay-life it will go waste as there was none else to enjoy it. But the venerable Ratthapala politely declined. Then, his father tried through Ratthapala's former wife to drag him into sensual pleasures but he remained firm and calm, and addressed her as sister. On being so addressed, she cried and fainted.

Then the venerable Ratthapala said to his father: "If there is food to be given, householder, then give it; do not harass me."

At last, the food was served, and Ratthapala came away after taking his meal.

Another chief disciple of the Buddha was Mahakaccana. He was the son of the chief adviser to King Pajjota of Ujjain, and in due course succeeded his father in that capacity. Having heard about the virtues of the Buddha, the king of Ujjain was keen to invite the Blessed One to his capital city. He sent a seven-man delegation, headed by Mahakaccana, to conduct the Buddha to the city. When the delegation met the Buddha to extend an invitation on behalf of their king, Mahakaccana was so moved by the personality of the Buddha that he immediately sought admission into the fraternity of monks. Thus, he returned to Ujjain only as a Bhikkhu. In due course, Mahakaccana attained Arahatship, and was known as the best exponent of the doctrine in brief.

Having become a lay disciple of the Buddha, King Bimbisara was keen that his chief consort, queen Khema, should also see the Blessed One, who was then staying in the Bamboo Grove. Being proud of her beauty and gold complexion, queen Khema did not want to see the Buddha, for, she feared that the Buddha would look down upon her bodily beauty. However, on hearing from a poet the praise of the Bamboo Grove, she was tempted to visit it. So she went to the Bamboo Grove. The Buddha was then resting by the side of a tree. What the queen saw there, opened her eyes. The Buddha, by mystic potency, conjured up a woman like a celestial nymph, who stood fanning Him. On seeing this, Khema thought that the Buddha had women around Him much more beautiful than herself. Then she observed that woman; in no time she passed from youth to middle age and old age, and lost all her beauty. Bewildered Khema thought, 'so will be my body also!'. Knowing her thought, the Buddha preached to her, she became sanctified. Later, Khema joined the Sangha and became known for her great insight. She was ranked as one of the foremost nuns by the Blessed One.

Ever since the building of a vast monastic complex by Anathapindika at Jetavana, Sravasti had become an important centre of Buddhism, and the Buddha often visited Sravasti. One of the greatest benefactors of the Buddha, after Anathapindika was Visakha, daughter-in-law of a rich merchant of Sravasti, namely Migara.

Visakha was the daughter of Dhananjaya, a rich merchant of Bhaddiya in King Bimbisara's territory. Both her father and mother were great devotees of the Buddha. Whenever the Blessed One visited Bhaddiya, Visakha also went along with her parents or other girls, to hear Him preach. When she was grown up, Visakha was married to Punnavaddhana, son of Migara, a wealthy merchant of Sravasti. Her husband's family favoured the Naked ascetics, and Visakha, who came from a Buddhist family, missed the Buddhist atmosphere to which she had been accustomed in her own house. Therefore, when the Buddha came to stay at Sravasti, she sought permission from her husband to invite the Buddha to the house. As her husband did not like to annoy her, he agreed. Accordingly, the Buddha came for the meals. Visakha's father-in-law, who was much more attached to the Naked ascetics, who also somehow persuaded to come and listen the Buddha's discourse. Hearing the Buddha, Migara realized that her daughter-in-law was on the right path. He also became a lay adherent. Migara was so much impressed by the devotion and piety of Visakha that he hailed her as his mother. Hence, Visakha came to be known as Migaramata. Later, when Visakha was blessed with a son, he was named Migara.

After the conversion of Visakha's in-laws, the wealth of the family was placed at Visakha's disposal to continue her pious donations. And she made the best use of it. Often, Lord Buddha and Bhikkhu Sangha took meals at Visakha's mansion. Once she experienced a little difficulty in informing the monks that the meal was ready. It had been raining, and the maid whom she sent to announce the hour of meals to them, seeing the monks standing uncloaked in the rain, thought they were Naked Ascetics, and not Bhikkhus, she returned to Visakha only to be told to go back. By the time, the maid came back, the monks had gone into their cells, and the servant thought the Vihara was empty and that there were no monks. Sometime after this, Visakha went to the Buddha, and finding appropriate time, she begged the Buddha for eight boons. The boons which she wished to offer throughout her life were: 1. Bathing clothes to the monks; 2. Meals to the visiting monks; 3. Meals to the resident monks; 4. Food to the sick monks; 5. Food to the monks who attend on the sick monks; 6. Medicine to the sick monks; 7. Gruel to the monks; and 8. Bathing robes to the nuns.

Visakha's generosity seemed to know no bounds. She not only supplied the material requirements of a large number of monks, but also occasionally visited the monastery to enquire about the welfare of the monks, and to tend the sick monks. One of her major benefaction to the Sangha was the erection of a magnificent Vihara at Sravasti. It so happened that one day, after listening to the sermon of the Buddha, she inadvertently left her costly necklace in the Jetavana. The venerable Ananda picked it and kept it aside safely. Later, when she came to know that Ananda had put it by for her, she thought that it would not be proper to wear it again. So she decided to sell it. But no purchaser could be found. There were only three ladies who had such a precious necklace. One of these was Visakha herself; the second was Mallika, the wife of Bandhula, the general of the Mallas; and the third was another Mallika, daughter of a great merchant of Benaras. Visakha herself paid the price, and asked the Buddha what gift she should give to the Sangha. He suggested a dwelling place for the monks at the East end. Pleased with this suggestion, Visakha soon began work on the monastery to the east of the city. The monastery built by Visakha, because of its location was popularly known as Puvarama. The Buddha sanctified Puvarama by spending as many as six rainy seasons there and enjoying generous hospitality of Visakha.

While King Bimbisara of Magadha had first become a lay devotee of the Buddha, and then inspired his queen Khema to come to the refuge of the Blessed One, two other kings, King Udena of Kosambi and King Pasenadi of Kosala were converted to the faith of the Buddha by their queens. King Udena was converted by his queen Samavati, who herself had been converted by Khujjuttara, one of her female slaves, and one of the most learned female lay disciple of the Buddha; and King Pasenadi or Prasenajit was converted by Mallika, his chief queen. Mallika herself appears to have been converted after listening to a discourse of the Buddha at Jetavana. Later, she through her frequent talk about the Buddha's teachings, influenced the king to come to the refuge of the Buddha. One day, it so happened, that consoling a man whose child had died, the Buddha said: "Dear ones, those who are dear, bring sorrow, lamentation and grief" the suffering that results from clinging to love. This conversation was reported to the King and he asked his wife, queen Mallika, whether it was really true that sorrow would result from love. "If the Buddha has said so, then it is so", she replied calmly.

The King demurred that she accepted every word

of the Buddha as a gospel truth. Thereupon, she sent a messenger to the Buddha to ask for more details, and then talked to her husband again. She asked the King whether he loved his daughter, his second wife, the crown prince, herself and his kingdom? Naturally, he confirmed this as all the five things were dear to him. "But if something happened to these five would he not feel sorrow, lamentation, and grief?", Mallika asked. Then the King realized the true meaning of what the Buddha had said. Having understood that, he said: "Very well, Mallika, continue to venerate the Buddha."

Thus inspired by Mallika, King Pasenadi visited the Buddha at Jetavana monastery and sought His blessings. Knowing the King's love for hunting and pleasure, the Buddha gave him an appropriate sermon on the fleeting nature of sensual pleasures, and said: "Our good or evil deeds follow us continually like shadows. That which is needed is a loving heart. Let your happiness depend, not upon external things but your own mind. Thus you will lay up a good name for distant ages".

From then onward, the King of Kosala became a lay disciple and a great supporter of the Buddha, and he built 'Punya sala' a big hall near his palace at Sravasti for the use of the Buddha for giving sermons to the town-folk.

At that time, the kingdom of Kosala was greatly terrorised by the robber Angulimala. It is said that his original name was Ahimsaka, and he was the son of the chief advisor to the King of Kosala. He was sent for his studies to Takshila, where he completed all his studies well. In fact, he outshone in studies all other students. His co-students, out of jealousy, conspired against him and poisoned the mind of his teacher that Ahimsaka wanted to kill him. Consequently, the teacher became suspicious.

He thought of a sinister plan to take revenge. At the end of Ahimsaka's course of study, the teacher asked Ahimsaka to bring him as reward, Guru dakshina', a garland of one thousand fingers of human beings. To repay his debt to his teacher, Ahimsaka was thus forced to adopt the life of a robber. He came back to Kosala; took up arms and went out to kill the required number of people. Soon, he devastated the whole region by killing the people who came his way, and formed a garland out of the fingers of his victims. Hence, he was called Angulimala, the man with a garland of fingers.

By and by, Angulimala had collected 999 fingers. One more finger, he thought, then the job is over. At that time, the Buddha was at Sravasti. One morning, the Blessed One saw the future of Angulimala, and set out in the direction of his region after His alms round in the city. Seeing the Buddha going that way, the people told the Buddha about the merciless murderer Angulimala and requested Him not to go towards the forest. But the Buddha remained silent, and proceeded forth as the Compassionate One was determined to save Angulimala from the henious crime of murdering his own mother.

In the meanwhile, Angulimala anxious to complete his target of 1000 fingers, scanned the roads from his hide-out and felt relieved on spotting a woman coming into the forest on the highway. He thought: "Well, with this woman's thumb I shall redeem my pledge." And seizing his weapons, he ran towards the woman. As he neared, he saw that the old woman was none else but his own mother and he hesitated. But again in his anxiety to redeem his pledge, he decided to murder his mother. Just then, he noticed a monk coming along the highway from the other side. So he changed his mind and the target. Seizing his sword and shield, Angulimala dashed in pursuit of the Buddha. Though he ran as fastest as he could yet he failed to overpower the Buddha. Thus utterly exhausted physically, Angulimala shouted loudly: "Stop, stop, you monk!" "I have stopped long ago. It is you, Angulimala,who should stop!". Unable to fathom the meaning of what the Buddha said, Angulimala again said somewhat in anger:

"While you are walking, O Monk, you say you have stopped; but now I have stopped, you say I have not stopped. I ask you, O Monk, what is the meaning of it ? Why do you say that you have stopped and I have not ?"

"Angulimala, I have stopped for ever, for, I have stopped harming any living being, but you have not stopped from doing harm to others. So do I say I have stopped, and you have not."

"Angulimala now understood the meaning why the Buddha asked him to stop. He realized that by his crime he has been only perpetuating his misery, his wandering in samsara. He threw away his weapons and the garland of fingers into a deep pit and prostrated at the feet of the Blessed One. Then he begged the Buddha to make him a monk. And out of boundless compassion, the Buddha said: "Come O monk!"—Lo the savage robber turned into a monk miraculously! Thus did the Buddha tame Angulimala and transform him into a saint.

The Buddha then, accompanied by Angulimala, returned to Sravasti and came to Jetavana where He was then staying. Next day, King Pasenadi, accompanied by five hundred armed men came to Jetavana. The Buddha was then in the midst of delivering a discourse to a vast audience. Interrupting His sermon, the Blessed One asked the King, "How is it great King, you appear so perturbed? Has any hostile king attacked your kingdom ?"

"It is not that, Lord. We come here seeking your blessing, so that we may succeed in putting Angulimala down. He goes on murdering people, and he wears their fingers as a garland."

"But, great king, if you see Angulimala transformed, having become a monk."

"In that case, Lord, I shall pay him reverence that is due to a monk. But, Lord, how can such a savage robber take to the life of virtue and self-restraint."

Just then, Angulimala was sitting not far off. The Blessed One extended his right arm, and said:"Great King, there is Angulimala". The King was visibly upset and disturbed. Observing king's fear, the Buddha said: "do not be afraid, great king, do not be afraid. There is nothing to be feared now."

Then the king calmed down. He went upto the venerable Angulimala and asked "Are you the robber Angulimala".

"Yes, great king."

The king Pasenadi then went back to the Buddha, prostrated at His feet, and then, sitting down reverently at one side, said : "Wonderful Lord, Wonderful Lord: One whom we could not subdue with weapons, the Blessed One has subdued him without weapons."

In due course, Angulimala became an Arahat through diligent spiritual efforts.

The story of the girl Patacara shows how the Buddha by His boundless compassion helped the afflicted, the destitute and the distressed. Patacara was the beautiful daughter of a very wealthy merchant of Sravasti. When she was sixteen years old, she took a wrong step and became involved in a love affair with a servant in her parents' house. And when her parents arranged her marriage with a young man of their choice, she eloped with her lover on the wedding day.The young couple went to live in a village far away from Sravasti. In due course, she became pregnant, and aware of the usual custom on such occasion, she begged her husband to take her to her parents' house. But her husband refused as he feared that her parents would torture him. Inspite of his objections, she set out for her parents' place. Her husband followed her begging her to return. But she would not listen to him. So they continued the journey. Before they could reach Sravasti, the birth-pains started, and soon a baby boy was born. As there was no more reason to go to her parents' house, they turned back and resumed their family life in the village.

After sometime, she became pregnant again. Again she expressed her wish to go to her parents' home. As her husband refused, she started off alone, carrying the child. Reluctantly, her husband also followed her.

On the way, a fearful storm arose with thunder, lightning and incessant rain. Just then her birth-pains started, and she asked her husband to find her some shelter.

When the husband was chopping down some saplings required for the shelter, a poisonous snake bit him and he fell dead instantly. Patacara waited for him in vain, and while alone she gave birth to her second child. Exposed to the rain and cold, she spent the night protecting her sons with her own body. In the morning, she came across the dead body of her husband. Wailing and lamenting, she continued her journey. So carrying her new born baby on her hip and leading the other child by her hand Patacara walked on until she reached the river Aciravati which was swollen on account of the rain. She felt too weak to wade across with both children. So she left the elder child on the bank and carried the new born baby across to the other side. Then she returned to take the elder child across. When she was mid-stream, an eagle saw the new born baby and mistook it for a piece of meat. It came swooping down and, inspite of Paracara's cries and screams, flew off with the baby.

When the elder boy saw his mother stop in the middle of the river and heard her loud yells, he thought that her mother was calling her and entered the river. Immediately, he was swept off by the strong current.

Thus in quick succession, within a day, Patacara lost her husband, and both sons. As a result of this triple tragedy, she lost her balance of mind, and wailing and lamenting she went on her way. As she came nearer to Sravasti, she enquired from a traveller about her family, and was shocked to learn that her parents' house had collapsed in the storm, killing both of them as well as her brother. The man pointed to a fire nearby which, he explained, was their funeral pyre. When she heard that, her grief became unbearable. She tore off her clothes, wandered around weeping and wailing, not knowing what she was doing or where she was going. In that condition, she somehow reached Jetavana where the Buddha was staying. The Blessed One saw Patacara coming from afar and instructed His disciples not to stop her, but to let her enter and come near him. As soon she was close to the Buddha, she regained her right mind and became aware of being naked. In her shame, she crouched upon the ground. One of the lay-followers, who was listening to the Buddha's discourse, threw her a cloak and she wrapped herself in it. Then she saluted the Blessed One and recounted her tragic story. The Buddha listened to her with compassion, and asked some of the women present to wash and clothe her, and give her food. Thereafter, the Buddha explained to her about the painful experiences she had gone through and the reasons for that. Patacara later joined the Sangha, and eventually gained sanctification, Arahatship.

There is another story of a girl called Kisa Gotami which shows how the Buddha could heal grief-stricken people and bring them out of their over-powering delusion.

Kisa Gotami lived in Sravasti. She came from a rich family, but was not very attractive. When married, her husband's family did not take to her kindly. But when Kisa Gotami gave birth to a baby boy, everything changed suddenly. Now she was happy and contented.

After a couple of years, however, a misfortune befell her. Her little son died suddenly. This was a great tragedy for her. She was very much attached to her child because he was the guarantee of her marital bliss and her peace of mind. In her grief, she lost her balance, and refused to accept the fact that the child was dead. She became obsessed with the fantasy that her child was only sick and that she had to get medicine for him.

With the dead child in her arms, she went from house to house asking for medicine to revive the child. At every door she begged, the people told her that no medicine would help now as the child was dead. But she did not understand the reality as she had resolved that the child was only sick. When she wandered hither and thither in search of the medicine, many laughed at her without compassion. But then she met a wise man who recognised that her mind was deranged because of grief. He advised her to visit the best physician, the Buddha, who was then staying in Sravasti.

As advised, she immediately ran to the Jetavana monastery, and arrived there in the middle of a discourse being given by the Buddha to a large congregation. Totally despairing and in tears, with the corpse of the child in her arms, Kisa Gotami begged the Buddha, "Lord, do you have medicine for my son." The Blessed One interrupted His teaching and replied that He knew of a medicine."

"What is that, Sir", she asked?

"Mustard seeds", the Buddha said, to the astonishment of all.

"My dear daughter, go and bring a few mustard

seeds?" the Blessed One said.

And when Kisa Gotami was about to leave, the Blessed One added the rider that the mustard seeds should be from a house where there has been never a death, no body has ever died.

Joyfully, Kisa Gotami ran to the city in search of mustard seeds. Wherever she asked for some mustard seeds, the people gladly promised to give her. But when she asked the second question: whether anybody had died in this house ? "Certainly", the people told her and related how they have lost their dear ones.

After going from house to house and hearing the same story everywhere, she finally realised that she was not the only one to be stricken by the death of a loved one, but this was the common fate of all. Having realized the truth, she took the corpse of her son to the cremation ground. Thereafter, she returned to the monastery. The Buddha asked whether she had brought any mustard seeds. "It is no longer necessary", my Lord, she said, and then went on to explain how she had been cured of her delusion by the Blessed One. Later, Kisa Gotami joined the Sangha and is said to have gained sanctification, Arahatship.

The Buddha did not force His views on others. He encouraged the people to think for themselves rather than blindly accepting His words or those of anybody else. On a certain occasion the Lord Buddha with a number of His disciples went to the village of the Kalamas. The Kalamas assembled, and did homage to Him and said that many saints and Brahmins have at different time visited them and explained their religious tenets, declaring them to be excellent but each abused the tenets of every one else, whereupon, they, the Kalamas, became perplexed as to whose religion was right and whose wrong; but as they had heard that the Buddha taught an excellent doctrine, they begged that they might be freed from doubt, and able to learn what the truth was.

The Lord Buddha answered, 'You were right to doubt, for after all, it was a doubtful matter. I say unto all of you, :

"Do not believe in anything merely because it is accepted by many or because it is based on some seemingly brilliant authority or some ancient and venerable tradition or some grand wishful thinking or, because it seems extraordinary, or because it has commendable connection."

Then the Kalamas asked, "What test should we apply in determining what is right, Sir?"

"Now what think ye, Kalamas? When greed arises within a man, does it arise to profit or to his loss."

"To his loss, Sir."

"When hatred arises within a man, does it arise to his profit or to his loss ?"

"To his loss, Sir.

"When delusion arises within a man, does it arise to his profit or to his loss ?"

"To his loss, Sir."

"Well then, Kalamas, what think ye ? Are these things profitable or unprofitable?"

"Unprofitable, Sir"

"Are they blameworthy or not ?"

"Blamesworthy, Sir".

"Are they censured by the wise or not ?"

"They are censured, Sir."

"If performed and undertaken, do they conduce to loss and sorrow or not ?"

"They conduce to loss and sorrow, Sir."

"So Kalamas, when you know for yourselves: These things are unprofitable, these things are blamesworthy, these things are censured by the wise, these things, when performed and undertaken, conduce to loss and sorrow,—then indeed you should reject them."

"But, Kalamas, when you know for yourselves: These things are profitable, they are blameless, they are praised by the wise, these things, when performed and undertaken, conduce to profit and happiness,—then Kalamas, you should accept them."

"So, Kalamas, I say unto you:

"Do not accept anything merely because it is accepted by many or because it is based on some seemingly brilliant authority or some ancient and venerable tradition or some grand wishful thinking or, it seems extraordinary, or because it has commendable connection; only when after proper observation, analysis and reflection, it is found in accord with reason and experience and is also conducive to happiness and general good, then accept it and live upto it."

Having thus made the Kalamas mentally responsive, the Buddha, gave a discourse on the Brahma Viharas, the four Divine Abodes—universal love, compassion, altruistic joy and equanimity. Then the Kalamas exclaimed with one voice, "Wonderful, Lord, most wonderful ! may the Lord accept us, from this day as His lay disciples."

The story of Siha, Senapati of the Licchavis of Vaisali, shows remarkable tolerance of the Buddha. General Siha, being the commander-in-chief of the Licchavi republic, had heard about the greatness of the Buddha from many Licchavi princes and other nobles. So he was keen to meet the Buddha. Before doing so, however, he sought permission of Mahavira (Nigantha Nathaputta), his teacher, but was dissuaded from doing so. In the ultimate, of his own he made up his mind to meet the Buddha, and ask some questions. Accordingly, one day Siha went to see the Blessed One. He started the discussion by recounting all sorts of allegations being levelled by the opponents against the Buddha. The Buddha calmly refuted one by one all the allegations, and explained the essence of His teachings. Overwhelmed by the sobriety and lack of malice shown by the Blessed One, Siha, then and there sought the Buddha's favour to accept him as a lay disciple. The Buddha was in no such hurry. He quite frankly told Siha that since he was an important member of a sect, he should carefully consider the pros and cons before changing his faith. The tolerance shown by the Buddha made further firm Siha's resolve to seek refuge in the Buddha-Dhamma. He again repeated his request of being accepted as a lay disciple, and added: "Venerable Sir, if any of the other sect were to secure me as a disciple, they would have organised a procession and announced loudly that, "Siha the General has become our lay follower". I was told that the Lord was a mind charmer, and that He gathered disciples for personal gain and glory, but now I see that the Lord tells me not to be in a hurry but to consider the matter deeply before becoming a lay disciple."

On being requested again, the Buddha accepted General Siha as a lay disciple but cautioned him not to antagonise his erstwhile co-religionists. He further urged him not to withdraw the regular alms which he had been giving to the Jaina monks.

On His preaching tours, the Buddha showed equal concern for the rich and the poor. In fact, on certain occasions compassion shown by Him towards the poor and the needy was a subject of critical comments. Once the people of Alavi, a village near Sravasti, invited the Buddha and the fraternity of monks for meals. On the appointed day, the Buddha arrived at Alavi. A poor farmer, who was keen to hear the Buddha, could not, however, reach the venue in time as he had to look for a lost bull and spent the whole morning in the search of it. Though tired and oppressed with hunger, he, without going home for food, came to the place where the Buddha was seated. After saluting the Buddha, the farmer stood aside. The Buddha asked the attendants whether any food is left. On knowing that it was there, the Buddha asked them to feed the farmer. After the farmer had finished his meal, the Buddha delivered His discourse which galddened the audience.

While dispersing, the monks began to talk about this sympathetic act of the Buddha. The Blessed One then explained that "no preaching could be understood by a person when afflicted with hunger."

At one time, a monk was suffering from dysentery

and lay where he had fallen down in his own excreta. The Blessed One on His usual round came to his residence accompanied by venerable Ananda, and asked: "What ails you, monk ?"

"I have dysentery, Lord."

Is there anybody to attend on you?

"No, Lord."

"Why is it that the fellow monks do not attend on you ?"

"Because I am useless to the other monks, they do not attend on me", said the monk.

Then the Buddha asked the venerable Ananda to go and fetch water. When he had fetched the water, the Buddha poured water on the sick monk while the venerable Ananda washed the sick monk all over. Then the Buddha taking him by the head and Ananda taking him by the feet, together they laid him on the bed.

The Buddha called all the monks staying there and advised them to attend on a sick monk whether he had attended on them or not. "Brethren, he who would wait on me, let him wait on the sick", said the Buddha.

There was a young man called Vakkali living in Sravasti. He often saw the Buddha on His rounds for alms, and was attracted by His bodily beauty. He became so much infatuated that he joined the Order just to be near the Buddha to admire His figure. And in the monastery, he followed he Buddha like a shadow, always gazing at the Blessed One's body. One day, the Buddha admonished him, saying, "Vakkali, what is the use of gazing all the time at this vile body of mine ? Whoever, Vakkali, perceives the Dhamma, sees the Buddha." But this admonition had no effect on Vakkali, and when the Buddha decided to go to Rajgir, Vakkali, also got up to go with Him. Then the Buddha firmly told him to stay back. Deeply disappointed, he returned to his cell, and after some time attempted to commit suicide by throwing himself from the top of a mountain. At this point, the Buddha miraculously appeared before him and saved him. Vakkali at last realised the folly of his ways, and devoted himself earnestly to meditation.

Sometimes the Buddha was abused and reviled. He won His opponents by patience and showing the right way to such people. One day, while going for alms from house to house in Sravasti, the Buddha approached the house of a Brahmin by the name of Aggika Bhardwaja.

The Brahmin, seeing the Blessed One coming at a distance, became angry and said: "Stay away, O Shaven headed One: There, stay, ye wretched monk ! Stay away, ye miserable outcast."

When he spoke thus, the Blessed One addressed him as follows: "Do you know, O Brahmin, who an outcast is, or the things that make a person an out-cast ?"

"No, Gotama, I do not know who an outcast is. Nor indeed do I know what things make a man an outcast."

The Brahmin having responded, the Blessed One spake as follows:

"The man who is irritable and bears hatred, who is wicked, detractive, perverted in views, and deceitful— know ye that he is an outcast.

"Whosoever in this world harms living beings, in whom there is no compassion for living beings—know ye that he is an outcast.

"Whosoever destroys or besieges villages and hamlets, and is known as an oppressor—know ye that he is an outcast.

"Be it in the village or in the forest, whosoever appropriates by theft what belongs to others or what has not been given—know ye that he is an outcast.

"Whosoever for the sake of some trifle, kills a man going alone on the road, and robs him—know ye that he is an outcast.

"Whosoever for his own sake, or for the sake of others, or for the sake of wealth, utters lies when asked as a witness—know ye that he is an outcast.

"Whosoever when questioned about what is good, counsels what is wrong and teaches in a concealing way—know ye that he is an outcast.

"No one is an outcast by birth—and no one is noble by birth; by deeds one becomes an outcast, by deeds one becomes a noble."

Aggika on hearing this, felt greatly ashamed for the abuse he had hurled against the Blessed One. He sought pardon from the Buddha and took refuge in the Triple-Gem, and became a life long devotee of the Buddha.

There was a haughty brahmin scholar, Bhardwaja. His wife had become a lay devotee of the Buddha, and she often gave vent to her devotion openly by praising the Buddha and glorifying His Teachings. Her husband never liked her praising the Buddha. One day when she repeated thrice, "Buddham Saranam Gachhami, Dhammam Saranam Gachhami, Sangham Saranam Gachhami", her husband lost his temper. He abused her, threatened her, and then dashed to the monastery where the Buddha was residing. The Blessed One was then in the midst of a large congregation, Bhardwaja just charged in, and shouted: "What must be slain to live in peace ?"

"Wrath must be slain, to live happily", replied the Buddha. This instant reply struck the brahmin like lightning, and he became sober. Then, he sat down and attentively listened to the discourse of the Buddha. He underwent so much spiritual transformation that he begged to be admitted into the Holy Order.

Now there was a cousin of Bhardwaja who was unhappy when his aunt had become a lay disciple of the Buddha. And when he heard that his uncle has gone a step further, and joined the Sangha, he became furious. In anger, he ran to the monastery where the Buddha was staying, and started showering upon Him the filthiest abuses. The Buddha remained silent. When finally the man had finished abuse, the Blessed One asked him, "Son, if a man declined to accept a present made to him, to whom would it belong?" And he answered: "In that case, it would belong to the man who offered it."

"Well said, my son," the Buddha replied, " I decline to accept the abuses that you have showered upon me, and request you to keep the same yourself." The abuser was non-plussed; he made no reply and went away.

Suppiya was a well-known brahmin ascetic with a large following. He was a good debator, and took pride in engaging in debate with the challengers of other religions. Once, the Buddha was going along the high road between Rajgir and Nalanda with a great company of monks. And Suppiya the mendicant too was going along the same road between Rajgir and Nalanda with his disciple, the young Brahmadatta. The teacher and the disciple were locked in a heated argument. While Suppiya speaking in many ways in dispraise of the Buddha, Brahmadatta was just doing the opposite—defending the Buddha and recounting His virtues in glowing terms. Some monks overheard their duel, and were amazed; some were hurt to hear the abuses about the Buddha.

Later, both the parties halted at the Ambalatthika rest house. Even there the strange dispute between the teacher Suppiya and his disciple Brahmadatta continued. The Buddha and the monks, witnessed the exchange but refrained from making any comment. Next morning, when some monks were discussing the outburst of Suppiya, the Buddha came upon the group, and on knowing the subject of discussion, He instructed the monks thus:

"Monks, if any one was to find fault with me, or abuse me, or the Dhamma or the Sangha, you should not on that account be offended, displeased or dejected. If you by any means become offended or perturbed, it will be to your harm. On the other hand, whenever people abuse and criticise, you should pause and consider whether what they say contains some truth or whether it is just slander and falsehood."

There is a bizarre incident in the life of the Buddha, of having been offered the hand of a maiden, Magandiya. When the Blessed One scornfully rejected the proposal, Magandiya who was very proud of her beauty, took it as an affront, and vowed to take revenge. Later, she married the king of Kosambi. And when in the course of His wanderings, the Buddha happened to visit Kosambi, Magandiya engaged a gang of anti-socials, who followed the Lord wherever He went on His alms round, showering upon Him filthy abuses. They also insulted and harassed the Buddha in every possible manner.

The venerable Ananda, who was with the Buddha, was so much upset, disturbed and distressed by the miscreants' abuses that he one day proposed to the Buddha that they leave the city forthwith.

"Where, Ananda, shall we go?"

"Lord, to some other place."

"If the people abuse us there, where shall we go?"

"To yet another place, Lord."

"Even there, if people abuse us, then?"

"To some other place again."

"Not that way Ananda, the Blessed One said, we must solve the problem where it has arisen."

The Buddha further said, "Ananda, do not despair. Let us endure with patience the vile words of the wicked men in the same way as an elephant on the battleground withstands the arrows from all directions. Moreover, this mischief will continue for a week only."

As predicted, the miscreants having failed to provoke

the Buddha realized their folly, and on the seventh day they prostrated before the Lord, seeking His forgiveness.

How the teachings of the Buddha spread to far flung regions, and how the monks endeavoured to preach the Dhamma notwithstanding the risks and hazards involved in doing so is very well reflected in the story of Punna of Sunnaparanta, a place somewhere on the west coast of India. Punna was a merchant and often went to sea on mercantile expeditions. During one of his voyages he had for companions some Buddhist merchants from Sravasti. He was very much impressed by their religious demeanour and progressive outlook. These merchants at night and at dawn recited some Pali suttas in a very sweet voice. On knowing that these were the words of the Buddha, he became keen to know more about the Dhamma. On his return, he straight away went to Sravasti, and listened to a discourse of the Buddha. On hearing that discourse, Punna was impressed so much that then and there he sought ordination as a monk. It was not long after that Punna through his intense spiritual practice gained sanctification, Arahatship. Then he thought, why not preach this marvellous Dhamma among his own people ? So he went to the Buddha, and sought permission to go to Sunnapranta and preach the doctrine. But the Blessed One knowing the violent nature of the people in that region thought of testing Punna's determination in carrying out the missionary work. The dialogue between the Master and the disciple on this occasion runs as follows:

The Buddha: The people of Sunnapranta are violent

and cruel, Punna. If they were to abuse and insult you, how would you feel ?

Punna: I would feel that the people of Sunaparanta are good and gentle people, since they are not striking me with their hands!

The Buddha: But if the men of Sunaparanta were to strike you with their hands, how would you feel?

Punna: I would feel that they are good and gentle people, since at least they are not hitting me with sticks.

The Buddha: But if they were to strike you with sticks, how would you feel?

Punna: I would still feel that they are good and gentle people at least they are not striking with a weapon and thus taking my life.

The Buddha: But if the men of Sunaparanta were to deprive you of your life, Punna, how would you feel?

Punna: I would still think they are good and gentle people, since they release me with so little pain from this body full of ordure.

"Good, good, Punna!", said the Buddha, you are endowed with the greatest gentleness and forbearance. Go and live in Sunaparanta, go and teach them the holy Dhamma, teach them how to be free, as you yourself are free."

Then, Punna, taking leave of the Buddha, went back to his homeland in Sunaparanta, and was successful in his mission of softening the violent and cruel inhabitants of Sunaparanta. He is said to have gathered around him 500 disciples.

The missionary life of Lord Buddha was not entirely a smooth affair. There was strong opposition to Him from the vested interests who thought that the Buddha had deprived them of their gain and honour. Some accused Him of being a parasite; living upon others and not earning His living by working for it. And some others spread the canard that the Buddha was bent on turning the women barren, by depriving them of husbands, who attracted by His spell, renounced household life. Unable to stem the tide of Buddha's popularity by such criticism, His rivals hatched a number of plots to discredit the Blessed One. Of these, the most sinister plot hatched by them was to tarnish the image of the Buddha through Cincha, a beautiful heretic wandering nun. She was instigated by a clique of the Buddha's opponents to organise a diabolical scheme aimed at destroying the honour of the Buddha.

This is how the wicked Cincha went about to achieve her evil design to defame the Buddha. Daily in the evening when the people of Sravasti returned from the Jetavana after hearing the discourse of the Buddha, she would go in the direction of Jetavana, wearing the best of clothes. And then she would spend the night in a hermitage of the heretics, close to Jetavana, and return to the city next morning at a time when the devotees went to the Jetavana monastery to pay their respects to the Buddha.

After about a couple of months when the people questioned her about her nightly visits, she began to say: "I spent the night with the monk Gautama in the fragrance chamber at the Jetavana monastery. Then she wrapped her belly with strips of cloth to pretend that she was pregnant, and went about saying: I have conceived a child by the Monk Gautama." Finally, when about nine months had elapsed, she tied on her belly a device made of pieces of light wood appropriately fashioned, and covered it with a silken cloth. Then, one evening when the Blessed One was preaching to a large assembly, she disturbed the sermon, and going just in front of the Buddha said sarcastically:

"Well, great monk, now you are preaching your doctrine to this great concourse of people. Yes, sweet is your voice, and attractive your lips. And you are the one by whom I have conceived and am in this advanced stage of pregnancy. Yet, you don't bother to provide me with the necessary maternity facilities. What a shame that you only know how to take your pleasure, and you don't know how to take care of the child you have begotten." Thus did Cincha slanderously revile the Buddha in front of a large gathering of devotees.

The Buddha stopped the discourse for a while, and said to her : "Sister, the truth or otherwise of what you have said now is something of which only you and I know."

"Yes, great Monk", retorted Cincha, "that you and I know it is certainly very well-known!" While saying so, she got agitated: began to tremble with anger: and the cords that tied the wooden device to her belly got loosened, and the wooden device fell upon her feet, cutting off both the toes.

On seeing this, the people cried out: "Fie upon you, you wretched woman! You falsely accuse the Enlightened One!" And then they beat her and drove her out of the Jetavana monastery.

The opposition to the Buddha from within the organisation came from none else but Devadatta, His jealous cousin. He had joined the Holy Order along with other Sakyan princes. Ambitious as he was, Devadatta wanted to be named as Buddha's successor which the Blessed One refused. Then Devadatta proposed that monks should follow stricter discipline than what the Buddha had prescribed. But the Buddha refused to make the proposed rules obligatory saying that any monk who wishes may follow these suggestions. Thereupon, Devadatta tried to create schism in the Sangha but he was not very successful as Sariputta persuaded most of the monks to come back. Having failed to achieve his object by peaceful means, Devadatta resorted to violent methods. Somehow, he had become a confident of Ajatsasatru, who had imprisoned his father, King Bimbisara, and usurped the throne of Magadha. Instigated by Devadatta, Ajatasatru sent assassins to kill the Buddha but they failed. In fact, over-powered by the compassion of the Buddha, they surrendered before the Buddha and became His disciples. Then in frustration, Devadatta tried himself to kill the Buddha. First, by letting loose a mad elephant, Nalagiri, which the Buddha tamed; and second time by hurling down a large rock, when the Buddha was resting at the foot of the Vulture Peak at Rajgir. The rock fell upon another rock and there it was entombed. However, a splinter falling from it injured a toe of the Buddha.

The most remarkable aspect of Lord Buddha's missionary life was that the means employed by Him to convert the people to His faith were the noblest.

He was kind, courteous and compassionate to all. He never sought to compel, but endeavoured to persuade others. 'He even made allowance for their weakness, varying in a thousand ways the means of impressing them; and when too inflexible and austere language might repel them, he had recourse to the more persuasive teaching of parables.' The Buddha was also against conversion through miracles. He had in fact, forbidden His disciples to exhibit psychic power in public.

Once a great merchant of Rajgir got made a precious bowl of sandalwood; tied it up at the top of a very high bamboo pole; and he proclaimed thus: "If there is any one sanctified and of psychic power, he may come through the sky and take this bowl." The merchant also declared his intention to follow the teachings of any one who proves his sanctification by coming through the air and lifting the bowl.

All the teachers of other religions and their disciples tried but failed to claim the bowl. Then, one day, when the venerable Pindola Bhardwaja was on his rounds for his alms in the city, he heard the story of the sandalwood bowl, and the inability of any one to claim it during the last seven days. Pindola was known for his psychic powers. He thought that it was a good chance to show his psychic powers as well as to convert the millionare. So he went through the air over the city, and lifted the bowl. When he came, with the precious bowl, to the monastery, he was followed by a large crowd who wished to see more miraculous feats. The Buddha heard the commotion in the monastery, and enquired the cause of it. On knowing that the reason for this large crowd in the monastery was the display of psychic powers in public by Pindola, the Buddha found fault with him, and rebuked him, saying:

"It is not suitable, Pindola, it is not becoming, it is not fitting, it is not worthy of a recluse, it is not allowable, it is not to be done. How can you, for the sake of miserable wooden bowl, exhibit a condition of further-men, a wonder of psychic power to householders ?"

Having rebuked him, the Lord addressed the monks, saying: "Monks, a condition of further-men, a wonder of psychic power is not to be exhibited to householders. Whoever should exhibit them, there is an offence of wrong doing. Break, monks, this wooden bowl; having reduced it to fragments, give them to the monks as perfume for ointment."

The Buddha further said:

"There are three miracles. The first is the miracle of power, in which extra-ordinary power is manifested, as in walking on water, exorcising devils, raising the dead and so forth. When the believer sees such things his faith may become deepened, but it would not convince the unbeliever, who might think that these things are done by the aid of magic. I, therefore, see danger in such miracles and I regard them shameful and repulsive. The second is the miracle of prophecy, such as thought reading, sooth saying, fortune telling etc. Here also there would be disappointment, for those too in the eyes of the unbeliever are no better than extra-ordinary magic. The last is the miracle of instruction. When any of my disciple brings round a man by instruction to rightly employ his intellectual and ethical powers, that is the True Miracle."

Notwithstanding His opposition to miracles, the Buddha was once Himself compelled to resort to a miracle. This happened at Sravasti, the capital of the Kosala kingdom, where the Buddha spent 25 rainy seasons and where He had the largest number of lay disciples. It is said that the king Pasenadi (Prasenajit) who had embraced the Dhamma and regularly visited the Buddha was confronted with a challenge from the rival sectaries to prove how the Buddha excelled them in miraculous powers. At the insistence of the King, the Blessed One responded to the challenge and the result was the greatest miracle. In the presence of a distinguished gathering at the Jetavana monastery, the Buddha in a series of miraculous episodes, created multiple representations of Himself, seated and standing on lotuses and causing fire and water from His body. Amazed by this miracle, the rival sectaries cried out," Let us run and take refuge in the hills, woods, groves and trees." When they were about to depart, the Buddha said: "Many people, tormented by fear, resort to hills, woods, groves, trees and shrines but that refuge is not secure. He who seeks refuge in the Buddha, the Dhamma, and the Sangha seeks refuge supreme. This indeed is the refuge secure."

After this great miracle, the Buddha is said to have visited the Trayastrimsa Heaven (Heaven of the Thirty-three Gods) where He preached the Dhamma to His mother, Mahamaya, and other Gods for three months. The Buddha descended on earth at Sankasya (Sankissa), in district Farrukhabad in Uttar Pradesh, where He was ceremonially received by the people.

There are two other miracles attributed to Lord

Buddha but they fall in somewhat different category. In the first case, on one occasion when the Buddha was staying in the forest near Vaisali, monkeys are said to have offered Him a pot of honey. In the other case, the Buddha tamed the rogue elephant let loose by Devadatta who wanted to kill the Buddha. This happened in the city of Rajagaha (Rajgir). When the Buddha, accompanied by Ananda was on His way to the monastery on the high road passing through the city, the mad elephant came running towards the Buddha. The people cried out, "Venerable Sir, this is the elephant Nalagiri, the ferrocious man-killer, please turn back."

The Buddha replied that no body can take the life of the Buddha, He continued the journey. As the terrible tusker came close to the Buddha, the Buddha projected powerful rays of all embracing love and compassion, and soon the elephant cooled down. Not only that, touched by the compassionate mind of the Buddha, Nalagiri knelt down, touching the feet of the Buddha with its trunk in reverence. Then it retreated, and remained fully tamed.

How far the Bhikkhu Sangha was a disciplined Order is very well illustrated by an incident when Ajatasatru, the king of Magadha, paid a visit to the Buddha at night in the monastery at Rajagaha (Rajgir) where the Blessed One was staying. It is said that Ajatasatru, after the murder of his father, Bimbisara, was unable to sleep. So to seek solace, on the advice of Jivaka, the noted physician, he decided to wait on the Buddha. The King left at night by torch-light mounted on an elephant and accompanied by Jivaka and large number of attendants. At that time, the Buddha was sitting with a large number of monks in the mango grove of Jivaka. Having gone quite far in the grove and not hearing any sound, the king was seized with a sudden fear, and said to Jivaka, "You are playing me no tricks ? You are not betraying me to my foes? How can it be that there should be no sound at all, not a sneeze, nor a cough, in so large an assembly." Jivaka assured him that there was no mischief afoot: "Go on, O king, go straight on. There in the pavilion hall the lamps are burning, and that is the Buddha sitting against the middle pillar, facing the east, with the Bhikkhus around Him." And when the king looked at the assembly seated in perfect silence, calm as a clear lake, he became at ease, and wished that 'his son might have such calm'. In the dialogue that follows the Buddha discourses on the fruits of the life of a recluse. At the end of which Ajatasatru sought pardon for his past sins and promised to follow the Dhamma in future.

There are certain futile questions which keep on agitating the minds of certain people. Such questions are : "How was the universe created, is it everlasting, is it finite or is it infinite and then again, "What Am I, who Am I , whence came my being, whither will it pass?" The Buddha considered such questions not only unimportant but was also a hindrance in the attainment of happiness, in spiritual progress. The dialogue between the Buddha and Malunkyaputta, a monk who showed more interest in speculative questions concerning the world than in his meditation, shows how the Lord taught the people to concentrate on spiritual progress rather than worry about futile philosophical questions.

Malunkyaputta had a restless mind and during his meditation he often pondered over the questions, such as Is the world finite or infinite? Is the soul identical with the body or not ? And so on. Not finding satisfactory answers to these questions, he one day went to the Blessed Buddha and after telling his problem, he said: "If the Blessed One will explain these matters to me I shall continue to follow the holy life under Him but if not I shall leave the Order and go away."

Admonishing the monk for attempting to blackmail Him, the Buddha said, Did I ever ask you, Malunkyaputta, to lead the holy life under me, promising to answer such questions?"

"No, ! Venerable Sir."

"Or did you tell me before joining the Sangha that you will not lead the holy life unless I explain to you such questions, the Buddha asked ?

"No, Venerable Sir".

Then the Buddha went on to say that whoever worries about such meaningless speculations that are not related in any way to spiritual progress, such a person is like one who refuses to be treated after being shot by a poisoned arrow, and says:

"I shall not allow my wound to be treated until I know who the man is who has shot me, to which caste he belongs—the brahmin, kshatriya, vaishya, the sudra; from which family he comes; whether he is tall, short or of medium height; whether he is dark in complexion, brown or yellowish; and what is type of bow and arrow he used with which he has struck me."

Such a person, Malunkyaputta, will surely die

without ever knowing these details. Even so, Malunkyaputta, if any one says: "I will not follow the holy life under the Blessed One unless He answers these questions such as whether the universe is eternal or not, etc. he would die with these questions unanswered by the Tathagata."

Then the Buddha explained that He teaches what is important to know, and not what is unimportant. The Buddha teaches the way to solve the problems of sorrow, suffering in this very life. He teaches what is useful, is fundamentally counted with the spiritual holy life, the Law of Piety that leads to full realization, Nirvana.

Once the Buddha was staying in a Simsapa forest near Kosambi. He took a few leaves into His hand, and asked His disciples: "What do you think, O Bhikkhus, Which is more? These few leaves in my hand or the leaves in the forest over here?"

"Sir, very few leaves are in the hand of the Blessed One, and many more indeed much more abundant leaves are there in this forest."

"Even, so, Bhikkhus, of what I have known I have told you only a little what I have not told you is very much more. And why I have not told you (those things). Because that is not useful..... not leading to Nirvana."

Having led for nearly 45 years, a very strenuous and selfless life in teaching the beauty of charity, the joy of renunciation, the need for morality and equality, the Great Buddha realized that time had come for Him to pass into Parinirvana.

6

MAHAPARINIRVANA

The Buddha had taken upon Himself a mission of converting and guiding the multitude on the Righteous Path. In doing so, He showed boundless compassion. He never cared for His personal comfort, and in order to save others, to show them the way to salvation, the royal road to Nirvana, He was on the move for eight months in a year, excepting the rainy season which He spent at any one place. And while on the move, He swept all before Him in the fervour of His conviction. His message cut across all barriers of caste, colour, sex or status, and His disciples, followers came from all walks of life, the rich, the poor, the high and the holy, the low and the lowly. All had equal opportunity to enter and walk the path, and attain the blessed state of Nirvana.

By the time Lord Buddha was about to lay down His mortal body, His personality and His teachings had penetrated deep in the hearts of the people. They used to consider it their good-luck and privilege to invite the Lord and the Bhikkhus for a meal. In fact, they vied with each other for this privilege. When the Buddha last came to Vaisali, and stayed in the mango-grove of Ambapali, the chief courtesan of Vaisali, she rushed to the place to pay her homage to the Blessed One. After welcoming the Buddha to her garden, Ambapali invited the Lord and the Bhikkhus for a forenoon meal next day at her residence, the Buddha accepted her invitation. On her way back, she met the Licchavi nobles who had also come to invite the Blessed Buddha but were forestalled by Ambapali. They entreated Ambapali and offered her a price, a hundred thousand rupees, for giving up the invitation but she politely declined on the plea that after waiting for a long time she had got a chance to serve the Buddha and would not like to miss this golden opportunity even if she was given Vaisali with all its lands. Next day, Ambapali offered the Blessed One and the community of monks the most delicious food with her own hands. After the meals, Ambapali donated her mango-grove (Ambavana) for the residence of the monks.

When the Buddha had stayed in Ambapali's mango-grove as long as He pleased, He went to the nearby village of Beluva to spend the rainy season. Here the Buddha became ill with a deadly disease which looked fatal but the Lord endured it with mindfulness, and overcame it by the force of will, as He did not want to attain Parinirvana without having assembled the monks once more. When, having recovered from illness, the Blessed Lord came out from His dwelling, the worried Ananda made enquiries about His health, the Buddha replied: "Now I am frail, old, aged, far gone in years, Ananda, I am now in the eightieth year and I have come to the end of my journey."

Then the venerable Ananda asked: "Any last

instructions about the community of monks, O Lord."

"What more does the community of monks expect from me, Ananda, I have preached the Dhamma in full: there is nothing, Ananda, which I have kept back. So, Ananda, let each of you make a refuge for himself, an island; and let that refuge be the Dhamma and nothing else."

Since the Buddha had completely mastered the Four Constituents of Psychic Power, He could have extended His life span and lived longer, but, it seems, the Buddha took a conscious decision not to prolong His life span.Therefore, He asked Ananda to assemble all the monks, residing in the neighbourhood, in the hall of the Mahavana at Vaisali. Addressing the monks assembled there on the Magha Full Moon day, the Blessed Lord said:

"I exhort you, O Bhikkhus, all component things are subject to decay. The time for Tathagata's Parinibbana is near. Three month hence, the Tathagata will pass away."

The Buddha further said:

"Now O Bhikkhus, I say unto you that Dhamma which I had made known to you should be well learned by you, cultivated, developed, preached and practised so that the life of Purity may last long for the welfare, for the good, for the benefit and happiness of all."

Next morning, the Buddha went on usual round for alms, and thereafter, He told Ananda that He was looking at Vaisali for the last time. Thereafter, He and Ananda left for Bhandagama. At this village, the Buddha spoke at length to the monks on morality, concentration and wisdom. Leaving Bhandagama, and passing through Hathigama, Ambagama and Jambugama, the Buddha arrived at the city of Bhoga, and dwelt there at Ananda Cetiya. He then, along with a large number of monks, proceeded to the city of Pava, and took up abode at the mango grove of Chunda, the blacksmith.

When Chunda heard that the Buddha was dwelling at his mango grove, he went to see the Lord, and invited Him for a meal at his house next day. One of the dishes prepared by Chunda was that of mushrooms. While the Buddha accepted this dish Himself, He asked Chunda to bury the remainder in a pit. After taking the meal, the Buddha became seriously ill but He bore the pain with equanimity, and continued the journey. On the way, He asked Ananda to spread His robe at the foot of a tree as He was exhausted and wished to rest. The Buddha further said: "I am thirsty, Ananda, will you bring some water." Ananda hesitated to bring water from the nearby stream as he thought that the stream water was fouled and spoilt by the cart wheels which had a little earlier passed that way. The Blessed One, however, again asked Ananda to go and bring water as He was thirsty. When the reluctant Ananda went near the stream he was amazed to see the clear and pure water. He expressed his joy at this marvel of Buddha's magical powers, and brought a jar full of water which the Buddha drank.

Continuing the journey further, the Buddha and the Bhikkhus arrived at the Sala grove of the Mallas in the vicinity of Kushinara. On reaching there, the

Blessed One spoke to Ananda, saying: "Ananda prepare for me the bed between the twin Sal trees, with the head to the north. I am weary, Ananda, and would lie down." Ananda did the Lord's bidding, and the Buddha lay down on the bed so prepared. Suddenly, the twin Sal trees broke out in full bloom, and the out of season blossoms dropped and scattered over the body of the Buddha. The sound of heavenly voices and heavenly instruments made music in the air, out of reverence for the Buddha. At that time, the venerable Upavana was standing before the Buddha, fanning Him. When the Lord asked Upavana to move aside and not stand in front of Him, Ananda was surprised and enquired the reason for this. The Buddha then explained that the innumerable deities had come from all directions to have a last glance of the Fully Enlightened One, who so seldom can be seen. But since Upavana was standing in front of Him, they could not see Him, hence He asked Upavana to move aside for the benefit of the deities.

Not knowing the reason why the Lord had chosen Kushinara as His last resting place, Ananda said, "Let not the Blessed One die in this wattle and daub town, in the midst of jungle. For Lord, there are great cities such as Champa, Rajagriha, Sravasti, Saketa Kosambi and Varanasi. Let the Blessed One die in one of them."

"Say not so, Ananda. Say not so, Ananda.

"Long ago, Ananda, there was a king by name Maha Sudarsana, a King of Kings, a righteous man who ruled in righteousness. This Kushinara, Ananda, was the royal city of King Maha Sudarsana, under the name of Kushavati."

"Go now, Ananda, and inform the Mallas of Kushinara, saying This day, in the last watch of the night, the final passing away of the Tathagata will take place".

Then Ananda went to inform the Mallas of Kushinara that the Blessed One had arrived there and would pass away in the last watch of the night. So informed, the Mallas came in large numbers to the Sal grove in the Upavana to have the last darshan of the Buddha.

Now at that time, there was a wandering ascetic dwelling at Kushinara. On hearing that the Buddha was in the town and was soon to attain Parinirvana, he thought it appropriate to go immediately, and have his doubts cleared before it was too late. Accordingly, he hastened to the Sala grove of the Mallas, and approached Ananda to let him see the Buddha. But the venerable Ananda answered him saying: 'Enough, friend Subhadda: Do not trouble the Tathagata. He is weary.' Yet a second and third time the wandering ascetic sought Ananda's permission but Ananda refused him saying that the Blessed One should not be troubled any more. The Buddha over-heard their talk, and He asked Ananda to let Subhadda to see Him as he wanted to inquire for the sake of knowledge, and not to cause trouble. Then, Ananda permitted the wandering ascetic to see the Buddha. The Compassionate Buddha heard Subhadda, cleared his doubts and taught him Dhamma. On hearing the true Dhamma from the lips of the Buddha, Subhadda was so much delighted that he immediately asked to be accepted as a Bhikkhu which the Buddha did. Thus Subhadda became the last monk to be directly ordained by the Buddha.

The last few hours were spent by the Buddha in useful counsels and instructions to Ananda:

"It may be Ananda, that some one among you will say: "Gone is the word of the Master: we have no longer any Master now! " But you must not so regard it. Ananda; for the Norm and Discipline taught by me, shall be your teachers when I am gone."

Then the Buddha addressed the monks and said: "If, O monks, there be any doubt as to the Buddha, or the Dhamma, or the Sangha, or the Path, or the Practice, you can question me now, so that you do not repent afterwards thinking—we were face to face with the Teacher yet we were not able to question the Tathagata before He attained Parinirvana."

When He spoke that, the monks were silent. For the second time, and third time the Buddha addressed the monks in the same way. And for the second and third time the monks were silent.

Then the Buddha again addressed the monks and said : "Perhaps it may be out of respect for the Teacher that you do not question me. Let a friend, O monks, intimate it to other another."

Still the monks were silent.

Thereupon, the venerable Ananda spoke to the Buddha as follows: "Wonderful, Lord ! Marvellous, Lord ! Thus am I pleased with the company of monks. There is not a single monk who entertains a doubt or perplexity with regard to the Buddha, the

Dhamma, the Sangha, the Path and the Practice."

"You speak out of faith, Ananda, with regard to this matter. But the Tathagata knows it for certain that in this company of monks there is not a single monk who entertains a doubt or perplexity with regard to the Buddha, the Dhamma, the Sangha, the Path and the Practice."

Then turning to the Bhikkhus, the Buddha gave His final exhortation: "Behold, O monks, I do remind ye, Subject to decay are all component things. Work for your salvation in earnest. Be ye lamps unto yourself."

These were the last words of the Blessed Buddha. Thus preaching, passed away the greatest of the world's religious teachers at the age of eighty on the Vaisakha Purnima day in 544 BC (or in 483 BC) lying between the two Sal trees.

The last rites of the Buddha were performed by the Mallas of Kushinara in a most dignified manner. For six days His body lay in state to enable His disciples to pay homage to the Master. On the seventh day, the Mallas carried the body of the Buddha in a procession to the Makuta-bandhana, where they used to hold their coronation ceremonies. There the Buddha was cremated with full honours under the guidance of Ananda, Anuruddha and Maha Kassapa, who had reached Kushinara by that time.

After the bone-relics had been collected by the Mallas, they kept the same in their Council-Hall and worshipped for seven days. Meanwhile, the news of Buddha's death spread far and wide, and soon there were many claims for the share of the relics. The relics were ultimately divided into eight parts and shared equally by the Mallas of Kushinara, Ajatasatru, the King of Magadha, the Licchavis of Vaisali, the Sakyas of Kapilavastu, the Bulies of Allakapa, Koliyas of Ramagrama, The Mallas of Pava, and a resident of Vethadipa. The vessel containing the remains of the Blessed One was taken by the wise Drona who was instrumental in dividing the relics to the satisfaction of all.

The site of the Buddha's Maha Parinirvana is in Deoria District, Uttar Pradesh. Kushinagar, as it is now known, is 55 kilometres from Gorakhpur. The site is marked by the Stupa and the Nirvana Temple, which were excavated in 1876. The 1500 years old Nirvana statue in the Nirvana Temple, which is again being worshipped, is 20 feet (6.1m) in length, and is executed out of one block of sandstone of mixed reddish colour probably from Chunar. It represents the Dying Buddha reclining on his right side with the face turned towards the west. It is placed on a 24 feet long brick throne with stone posts at the corners. An inscription of fifth century AD on the throne records that the statue was the appropriate gift of the Mahavihara-Svamin Haribala and that it was fashioned by 'Dinna'. The reclining Buddha image is said to be on the very spot where the Lord Buddha breathed His last.

7

THE DHAMMA : TEACHINGS

1. THE TRIPITAKA

During His long ministry of forty-five years, the Buddha had preached, and repeated His Teachings time and again in a systematic manner with extreme care and accuracy. These Teachings were preserved fully in the retentive memory of His illustrious disciples, and the same were also transmitted orally from generation to generation till they were committed to writing a few centuries later.

At the time of the Mahaparinirvana of the Buddha, only two of His five most prominent disciples, Ananda and Anurudha, His cousin brothers, were present. Sariputta and Maha Moggallanna had predeceased the Buddha, and Maha Kassapa was still on his way to Kushinara. During the walk he happened to meet a naked ascetic who was coming from Kushinara. Maha Kassapa asked the ascetic whether he had heard any news about his teacher, the Buddha. Affirming that he had, the ascetic said: "The recluse Gotama had passed into Nibbana a week ago."

On hearing this news, some of the monks

accompanying Maha Kassapa lamented and wept, saying: "Too soon the Blessed One has passed into Nibbana." But there was an old monk, Subhadda by name. He was ordained in old age and was a bit lax in discipline. He addressed the other monks and said: "Enough, friends! Do not grieve, do not lament! It is good we have got rid of that Great Ascetic who used to trouble us by telling us: "This is befitting, that is not befitting !" Now we can do what we like." Though perturbed by this remark, Maha Kassapa kept quiet, and continued the journey.

After the cremation of the Buddha, Maha Kassapa returned to Rajagaha (Rajgir). He also brought to King Ajatasatru his share of the relics of the Buddha. Having presented the same to the King, Maha Kassapa turned his thoughts to the preservation of the Buddha's spiritual heritage, the marvellous Dhamma. He proposed to hold a Sangiti, Council by which the Teachings of the Buddha could be reliably fixed and codified. When he shared his thoughts with the other monks gathered at Rajagaha, they readily agreed with him. Accordingly, the First Buddhist Council, consisting of five hundred selected Arahats, met at Rajagaha. First of all, at this Council, which was presided over by Maha Kassapa himself, the texts of the monastic discipline were recited by the venerable Upali, an authority on the Vinaya, and the same were, after due deliberation, confirmed by the Council. Thereafter, on being requested by Maha Kassapa, the venerable Ananda, the most devoted disciple and personal attendant of the Buddha for over twenty-five years, recited all the Dhamma texts which were later compiled in the

Five Collections (Nikayas) of the Sutta Pitaka. These Suttas, therefore, invariably begin with the words 'Thus have I heard' or 'So it was heard by me'. This is how the Teachings of the Buddha were codified and given a definite shape within three months of the Mahaparinirvana of the Buddha.

The Teachings of the Buddha were rehearsed again at the Second Council held at Vaisali after about a century of the passing away of the Buddha. They were further rehearsed and edited by the Third Council held at Patna (Pataliputra), in the third century BC. Finally, the Pali Canon was compiled in the form of books in Sri Lanka in 83 BC, where the fourth Buddhist Council was held for this purpose.

Since Lord Buddha spoke in Pali, the language of Magadha and adjoining territories at that time, the Pali Canon is regarded as the most authentic version of the Buddha-Word. Thanks to the devotion and dedication of Ven. Jagdish Kashyap, India now has the entire Pali Canon in Devnagari script. The 41 volumes of about 400 pages each prepared under his Editorship were published by the Pali Publication Board, Nava Nalanda Mahavihara, Nalanda, during the period 1956-1961.

The Pali Canon is commonly referred to as Tipitaka (Skr:Tripitaka), i.e. 'Threefold Basket'. The three Pitakas or 'Baskets of the Law' are:

1. The Vinaya-Pitaka or Discipline Basket.
2. The Sutta-Pitaka or Sermon Basket.
3. The Abhidhamma or Teaching Basket.

The Vinaya Pitaka comprises of Sutta Vibhanga (Parajika and Pacittiya), Khandhakas (Maha Vagga and Culla Vagga) and Parivara. It mainly deals with 227 rules of conduct which the Buddha promulgated, as occasion arose, for the future discipline of the order of monks (Bhikkhus) and 311 rules for nuns (Bhikkhunis). It describes in detail the gradual development of the Sangha. An account of the life and ministry of the Buddha is also given. It also reveals some important and interesting aspects of ancient Indian history, customs, traditions and arts, etc.

The Sutta Pitaka consists chiefly of discourses, delivered by the Buddha on various occasions. There are also a few discourses delivered by some of His distinguished disciples such as Sariputta, Moggallana and others included in it. The sermons embodied therein serve as moral guides. The Sutta Pitaka is divided into five Nikayas (groups or collections).

The Digha Nikaya "long collection" has 34 long sermons arranged in three vaggas or series, called the Silakhandhavagga, the Mahavagga and the Pathikavagga.

The Majjhima Nikaya is the collection of middle length sermons. It has 152 Suttas which are arranged in fifteen vaggas, roughly classified according to subject.

The Samyutta Nikaya 'collection of Suttas divided into groups' has in all 2941 suttas, classed in 56 Samyuttas in the five series or vaggas.

The Anguttara Nikaya has eleven Nipatas (groups). Each Nipata is divided into vaggas, which contain ten or more Suttas. The anga 'uttar' means 'one number in addition'. Thus the first Nipata deals with single things and is followed by groups of two and so on, upto group eleven. The Anguttara Nikaya (Book of Gradual Sayings) has 2308 suttas divided into 174 vaggas.

The Khuddaka Nikaya "collection of short texts" contains the following fifteen independent books :—

(i) Khuddaka-Patha—appears to have been compiled to serve as a hymn book for daily worship.

(ii) Dhammapada—is a collection of 423 stanzas grouped in 26 vaggas, covering all aspects of Buddhist ethics and philosophy.

(iii) Udana is an utterance that a saint utters in the bliss of his emancipation or in appreciation of a sublime state. This book contains 80 such utterances of the Buddha.

(iv) Itivuttaka—is a collection of 112 short suttas. All the suttas are introduced by "Thus has been said by the Blessed One, thus I have heard."

(v) Suttas Nipata—has 73 suttas, divided into five vaggas, in verse with occasional introductions. Some of the suttas are the most beautiful in the entire Buddhist literature.

(vi) Vimana-Vatthu—has 85 poems in which beings who have been reborn in the heaven explain the acts of merit that led to their reward.

(vii) Peta-Vatthu—This book has 51 poems which are the stories of Petas or the beings condemned for their former misdeeds to a wretched existence as ghosts and evil spirits.

(viii) Thera-gatha—This book has verses expressing joy over spiritual accomplishments by 264 monks (Bhikkhus).

(ix) Theri-gatha—A similar collection of poetic expressions by about 100 nuns (Bhikkhunis).

(x) Jataka—A collection of 547 stories of the previous existence of the Buddha. The introductory part of the commentary, known as the Nindana-Katha, gives a life sketch of the Buddha down to the presentation of the Jetavana monastery at Sravasti.

(xi) Niddesa—It has two parts (i) Maha-Niddesa, a commentary on the Atthaka-vagga of the Sutta- Nipata, and (ii) Culla-Niddesa, a commentary on the Parayana-vagga and Khaggavisana-Sutta of the same work.

(xii) Patisambhida-magga—It contains an analysis of various concepts, knowledge, the practice of breathing in meditating, etc.

(xiii) Apadana—A collection of previous lives of the Buddhas and some Bhikkhus and Bhikkhunis.

(xiv) Buddhavamsa—An account of the history of the twenty-four previous Buddhas as well as Gautama the Buddha.

(xv) Cariya-pitaka—It has thirty-five selected tales from the Jataka, in verse, to illustrate seven of the ten paramitas (perfections) attained by the Buddha.

The Abhidhamma Pitaka contains the profound philosophy of the Buddha's Teaching. It has the following seven books:

(i) Dhammsangani—It deals with the enumeration of the factors of existence.

(ii) Vibhanga—It consists of 19 independent treatises (Vibhangas) giving further analysis of the factors of existence.

(iii) Dhatukatha—In it the mental elements and their relations to other categories are discussed.

(iv) Puggalapannati—It describes individuals especially according to their spiritual attainments.

(v) Kathavathu—It gives analysis of the points of controversy among the eighteen early sects and their reputation.

(vi) Yamaka—It gives an analysis of psychological subjects arranged as pairs of questions.

(vii) Patthana—This gigantic work gives an analysis of the causation and the relationship of things in 24 groups.

2. WHAT IS NIRVANA ?

The Highest Goal in Buddhism is the attainment of Nibbana or Nirvana. Therefore, let us first see, what is Nirvana ?

Since the word 'Nirvana literally means 'blowing out', as of a lamp, some scholars define Nirvana as a state of nothingness, annihilation of all activities, extinction of everything. But this interpretation is not correct. Nirvana is extinction, yes, but it is the extinction of lust, greed, craving, hatred and ignorance. "The whole world is in flames", says the Buddha.[1] "By what fire is it kindled ? By the fire of lust, hatred and ignorance; by the fire of birth, and age, death, pain lamentation, sorrow, grief and despair it is kindled."

Once the venerable Radha asked the Blessed One: "Pray Lord, what for is Nirvana ?" "Nirvana means freedom from passions", replied the Buddha.[2] "But, Nirvana—Lord—what is the aim of it"? Rooted in Nirvana, the righteous life is lived, Nirvana is its goal, Nirvana is its end." Thus, Nirvana is another name for righteous life. It is the blessed state of freedom from desire, of freedom from greed, hatred and delusion.

Some scholars equate Nirvana with moksha or union with God or Brahma after death, or merging of an individual soul in the universal soul. Such a view is also not correct. Since Buddhism denies a soul as well as the Supreme Being, such an interpretation is simply not tenable. Unlike moksha after death, "Nirvana the highest bliss", says the Buddha, "is attainable in the present life, in this very body, with the sense impressions and its thoughts and ideas."

At another place, the Buddha says:[3]

"Enraptured with lust, enraged with anger, blinded by delusion, overwhelmed, with mind ensnared, man aims at his own ruin, at the other's ruin, at the ruin of both parties, and he experiences mental pain and grief. But if lust, anger and delusion are given up, man aims neither at his own ruin, nor at the other's ruin, nor the ruin of both parties and he experiences no mental pain and grief. Thus is Nibbana immediate, visible in this life, and not merely in the future."

That Nirvana is something that can be achieved and enjoyed in this very life is evident from the life of the Buddha whose entire ministry of 45 years was after He had realized Nirvana. Further, many of the Buddha's disciples, who like the Blessed One, had attained Nirvana, speak about it in positive terms, such as, bliss, happiness, tranquility and emancipation.

In fine, Nirvana is positive and transcendental in nature. As says Ven. Narada, "From a metaphysical standpoint Nibbana is deliverance from suffering. From a psychological standpoint Nirvana is the eradication of egoism. From an ethical standpoint Nirvana is the destruction of lust, hatred and ignorance."

Of course, there are two aspects of Nirvana. When Nirvana is realized in this life with the body still remaining, such as the Buddha, or an Arahat living, it is called Sa-upadi-sesa-nibbana. And when an Arahat attains Nirvana, after the dissolution of the body, it is called An-upadi-sesa-nibbana.

3. THE PATH TO NIRVANA

The Noble Eightfold Path is the fountainhead of the Buddha's Teachings. It is the Path to Nirvana. This Path[4] comprises of:

1. Right Understanding: free from superstition and delusion.

2. Right Thought: high and worthy of the intelligent, earnest man.
3. Right Speech: kindly, open, truthful.
4. Right Conduct: peaceful, honest, pure.
5. Right Livelihood: bringing hurt or danger to no living thing.
6. Right Effort: in self-training and in self control.
7. 'Right Mindfulness: the active, alert mind.
8. Right Concentration: earnest meditation to attain one-pointedness of mind.

Of these eight steps of the Noble Eightfold Path, the first two are grouped under the heading of Wisdom; the following three under Morality, and the last three under Concentration. But according to the order of development, the sequence is as follows: Morality (Sila), Concentration (Samadhi), and Wisdom (Panna or Prajna). These three stages are closely inter-related. Morality is the foundation of the life of righteousness. Without moral culture there cannot be meditation or mental culture, and without mental culture there cannot be wisdom. So, for gaining enlightenment and attaining Nirvana one has to tread the Noble Path of Sila, Samadhi and Panna.

The first step on the royal road to Nibbana or Nirvana is the observance of the Five Precepts(Pancha Sila), which are the core of Morality in Buddhism. The Five Precepts are in essence the combination of Right Speech, Right Action and Right Livelihood. The diligence observance of the Five Precepts (Pancha Sila), viz. Not to injure or kill; Not to steal; Not to indulge in lust; Not to speak untruth; and Not to take intoxicants, is the best way to avoid all sin and to purify one's mind. In brief, "the practice of morality (Sila) consists in the observance of all moral precepts; in feeling fear, shame and remorse at the smallest violation of any of them; in not giving room for blame or disgust; in practising those deeds which lead to moderation and contentment".

After securing firm foothold in Morality, one can move forward to take the second step of Concentration (Samadhi) which includes Right Effort, Right Mindfulness, and Right Concentration. By Right Effort, is to be understood a vigorous mental application by which a person, on the one hand, avoids and overcomes any evil thoughts, and on the other hand, develops and maintains good thoughts and urges. Right Mindfulness means constant wakefulness of the mind, that is, an alert awareness or contemplation of all bodily actions or movements. And Right Concentration (Samadhi) is the practice of meditation or taming the mind which ultimately leads to Nirvana.

There are two kinds of meditation in Buddhism. One form is Samatha, calm or development of mental concentration. Its aim is to develop the concentration of mind to the limit of one-pointedness and perfect tranquility which culminates in a series of mystic states or mystic experiences. Of the meditative practices suggested by the Buddha, meditation on the Four Sublime Abodes or Divine Abodes (Brahmaviharas) is considered the most helpful as by constantly meditating on these virtues one actually becomes perfect. The four divine abidings are: Loving-Kindness (Metta),

Compassion (Karuna), Sympathetic Joy (Mudita), Equanimity (Upekkha). Metta teaches fellow-feeling towards all living beings whereas Karuna is especially directed towards unhappy and afflicted beings. Mudita implies the feeling of happiness in the happiness of all. And equanimity is that faculty which enables a person to maintain the same attitude in all circumstances, favourable or unfavourable pleasant or unpleasant and delightful or sorrowful.

The other form of meditation, called Vipassana, is specifically Buddhist and is directly related to the Path of Deliverance. It was discovered by the Buddha at the time of His Enlightenment. Vipassana means a special kind of vision, observation of reality within oneself or to see things as they really are. By exposing the truth of impermanency, and unsubstantial nature of all material and mental phenomena of existence (anicca, dukkha, anatta), Vipassana ultimately leads to the complete liberation of mind, to the realization of the Ultimate Truth, Nirvana.

Having attained perfection in Samadhi, one reaches the final stage of Wisdom (Panna), that is, he has clear understanding of all the unwholesome actions, which are rooted in greed (lobha), hatred (dosa) and delusion (moha) as well as the wholesome actions. His mind becomes pure, is free from lust, free from ill-will; is full of kindness and compassion. He has reached his goal, and is on the threshold of Nirvana.

The road to Nirvana is not smooth; there are a number of hinderances, obstacles which one has to cross. The ten major Fetters[5] that come in the way of attainment of Nirvana are :

1. Self-illusion or belief in a permanent self, ego.
2. Scepticim or irrational doubts.
3. Attachment to rituals and superstitions.
4. Craving for sensual enjoyment.
5. Ill-will.
6. Craving for existence in Fine Material Worlds.
7. Craving for existence in Worlds without Material Form.
8. Conceit.
9. Restlessness.
10. Ignorance.

The progress of the pilgrim on the road to Nirvana depends on the breaking of these ten fetters or impediments, as they are called. One who is freed from the first three fetters of self-illusion, scepticism and attachment to rituals and superstitions, has reached the first stage of purification and realization. He has unshakable faith in the Buddha, the Dhamma, the Sangha, and is incapable of breaking the Five Moral Precepts. He is called Sotapanna or Stream Enterer, and will be born seven times at the most, that too not in a state lower than human being.

The second stage is reached when the pilgrim has overcome the fourth and fifth fetters of Sensual Lust and Ill-Will. He is called Sakadagami or Once-Returner, that is, he will be born only once more, and thereafter reach Holiness. An Anagami or Non-Returner is the one who is wholly freed from the first five fetters which bind one to rebirth in the Sensuous Sphere; after death, he will be reborn in the Fine Material Sphere and achieve the goal.

Finally, when the person is freed from all the ten fetters, including craving for material and immaterial existence, conceit or pride, self-righteousness, restlessness, and Ignorance, he attains Nirvana, the highest goal in Buddhism. He is the Arahat, the Holy One. He is the peaceful one, freed from rage, from sorrow, and from longing; he has passed beyond birth and decay.

4. THE LAW OF KARMA

According to the Buddha, the Universe is one eternal process, and there are five orders or processes (Niyamas) which operate in the physical and mental realms. These five orders are:

1. Utu Niyama, the order of physical laws, for example, the phenomena of change of seasons.
2. Bija Niyama, the order of germs and seeds, for example rice produced from rice-seed, sugary taste from sugarcane or honey etc.
3. Kamma Niyama, the order of moral laws, namely, good deeds lead to good results, and bad deeds to bad results.
4. Citta Niyamas, the order of mind or psychic laws, namely, the process of conciousness.
5. Dhamma Niyama, the order of the norm, the natural phenomena occurring at the advent of the Buddha.

All mental and physical phenomena in the world

could be explained by these all-embracing five orders or processes which are laws in themselves. Of these, the Law of Karma or the order of moral law, is the most important. The Pali term Kamma literally means action or doing, but in the theory of Kamma it covers volitional acts by body, speech and thought. Volition may be good or bad, just as desire may be good or bad. So Kamma or Karma constitutes both good and evil deeds.

Some thinkers are of the view that "Whatsoever happiness or pain or natural feelings a person experiences, all that is the creation of a Supreme God." This idea was not acceptable to the Buddha.[6] He argued, "if that is so, men become murderers, thieves, unchaste, liars, slanderers, abusive babblers, covetous, malicious and perverse, owing to the creation of a Supreme God." Further, "If God is Omnipotent and is also the efficient cause of creation, then because of this man cannot have any desire to do anything, nor can he have the will to do anything or to put forth any effort. Man must remain a passive creature with no part to play in the affairs of the world."

"Reap as you sow", says the Buddha. In other words, Man shapes his own destiny. It all depends on him whether to create painful, pleasurable or blissful life. The law of Karma is the law of cause and effect. As the law of cause and effect is universal, so is the law of Karma. Good deeds will naturally result in good fortune and happiness, and the bad deeds otherwise. In brief, we ourselves are responsible for our own happiness and misery. We are the architects of our own fate. The Buddha did not believe that Stars can change the course of life. His view was that 'self effort' not 'stars' can mould one's destiny. He says, "The fool may watch for lucky days, yet luck he shall always miss. Luck itself is luck's own star, what can mere stars achieve."

The Karma doctrine is also an essential feature of Hinduism. But there is a vast difference in the Law of Karma enunciated by the Buddha and the Law of Karma preached by Brahminism. In the Brahmanical theory, a man's present life is determined by the actions in his previous life, and he can do nothing to change the course of suffering and pain in this life. According to Buddha, a man can change his present life with the dint of his labour and right efforts. In the Buddhist Law of Karma, man's environments, and not hereditary connections, are important. In Hinduism, the law of Karma has been taken to be a punitive law or the law of retribution but Lord Buddha was opposed to this static view. He considered the doctrine of past Karma as the sole regulator of present life as an iniquitious doctrine. He says:

"O Bhikkhus, if any one were to say that man must reap according to his deeds, in that case O Bhikkhus, there is no religious life, nor is any opportunity afforded for the entire extinction of misery."

"But if any one says O Bhikkhus, that the reward a man reaps accords with his deeds, in that case O Bhikkhus, there is a religious life and opportunity afforded for the entire extinction of misery."

Hence, the Buddha's law of Karma is essentially related to the present life. That being so, 'it gives consolation, hope, self-reliance and moral courage to a person to change his life for the better; and it validates his effort, kindles his enthusiasm.'

5. NO-SOUL DOCTRINE

Anicca, Dukkha and Anatta, better known as the 'Three Characteristics' form the essential basis of the Buddha's Teachings. Here we will confine our attention to Anicca and Anatta; Dukkha (suffering) having been already discussed as part of the Four Noble Truths. The Anicca, impermanence, transience or transitoriness doctrine implied that in this world all things are changing, are in a perpetual flux. There is nothing, either divine or human, either animate or inanimate, either organic or inorganic, which is permanent or stable, unchanging or everlasting. In other words, all conditioned things or processes are transient or impermanent (sabbe sankhara anicca). Impermanence of the living individual is best described by the formula—being is becoming. In this sense, a being of a past moment has lived, but does not live nor will he live. The being of future moment will live but has not lived nor does he live; the being of the present moment does live but has not lived and will not live. In short, a human being is always changing, always growing. He is not the same at two different moments of his life. What is true of a human being, the same is true of all other animate and inanimate things. There is nothing fixed in the universe. Nothing is permanent in the universe but change. If things were not subject to continual change but were permanent and unchangeable, the evolution of all life from one kind to the other and the development of living things would have come to a dead stop. Had the law of change not been there, the world would have been static, not worth living. But it is not so, change is inherent in every thing.

The belief about Soul, Ego or Atman as a permanent and everlasting entity is part and parcel of theistic religions. In the Brahmanic religion, it is held that the soul does not die with the body but it flies away, and takes birth in another body when it comes into being. The Buddha denied this eternalist view. According to him, there is nothing permanent, unchanging entity in the human body which can be called soul or self. In His second sermon at Sarnath, a few days after Turning the Wheel of Law, the Buddha said[7]:

"The material form, O monks, is not the self. If material form were the self. O monks, this material form could not be subject to sickness, and a man should be able to say regarding his material form: My body shall be so and so; my body shall not be so and so. But inasmuch, O monks, as material form is not the self, therefore, material form is subject to sickness and a man cannot say, This is mine, this I am, this is myself."

After giving detailed exposition in the same manner about all the component elements, viz. Feeling, Perception, Mental Formations and Consciousnes, the Buddha goes on to say:

"What do you think of this, O monks, is material form permanent or impermanent ?"

"Impermanent, O Lord."

"But that which is impermanent, is it sorrow or joy ?"

"Sorrow, O Lord."

"But, that which is impermanent, full of sorrow, subject to change, is it proper to regard that as:, This is mine, this I am, this is my self ?"

"Indeed, not that, O Lord."

"Therefore, O monks, it must be regarded, according to reality, form is not my self, feeling is not my self, perception is not my self, mental formations are not my self, consciousness is not my self."

According to the Buddha, a being is a combination of Five Aggregates consisting of Mind and Matter (Nama and Rupa). The mental phenomena (Namakkhandha) consists of the Sensation, the Perception, the Volitional Activities, and Consciousness. The matter (Ruppakkhandha) primarily consists of earth (solidity), water (fluidity), fire (heat), and air (motion). All the mental and physical phenomena do not singly or collectively constitute any self-dependent Entity or Personality (Atta), nor is there to be found any such entity apart from them. Further, the so-called Individual existence, the combination of Mind and Body is constantly becoming and passing away. A personality, being in reality a Santati, a flux of mental and physical phenomena does not exist in the ultimate sense. When the water of ocean takes a particular shape, we call it a 'wave,' but there is no entity behind it except the particles of a wave water. As the Buddha says, "the sameness is constituted by continuity just as we speak of the identity of a river or a fountain, though the water is continually changing; of the identity between the flame of a lamp at one moment and that at another moment, although different particles of the wick and oil are consumed in succession."

In fine, Buddhism does not deny the existence of a personality in an empirical sense. It, however, shows that it does not exist in an ultimate sense. A modern Buddhist scholar, Walpola Rahula says:

"According to the Buddha's teaching, it is wrong to hold the opinion 'I have no self' (which is the annihilationist theory) as to hold the opinion 'I have self' (which is the eternalist theory), because both are fetters, both arising from the false idea, 'I AM'. The correct position with regard to the question of Anatta is not to take hold of any opinions or views, but to try to see things objectively as they are without mental projections, to see that what we call 'I' or 'being' is only a combination of physical and mental Aggregates, which are working together interdependently in a flux of momentary change within the law of cause and effect and that there is nothing permanent, everlasting, unchanging and eternal in the whole existence."

Another modern Buddhist scholar, Anagarika Lama Govinda says: "What the Buddha denied was unchangeable personal soul or ego-entity, because this would mean that each being would be eternally separated from all other beings, incapable of growth, development of perfection. To Him the human soul was a living, growing organism, a dynamic force which from life to life, continued on its self-chosen course, never the same, not even for two consecutive moments, and yet forming one continuous chain of action and reaction, i.e. an organic unity an 'individual' in the sense of a consciously evolving self-directing force."

6. DEPENDENT ORIGINATION

One of the fundamental teachings of the Buddha is that in this world 'nothing happens' 'without a cause'. This principle of 'cause' and 'effect' teaching the conditionality and dependent nature of all physical and mental phenomena, constituting existence is known as 'Causation' or 'Dependent Origination' (the Paticca Samupadda). This doctrine 'shows that the whole world is subject to the law of cause and effect or action and reaction. There is nothing in the universe that is causeless and unconditioned. The basic principle of the Causation was summed up by the Buddha like this:

When this is, that is

When this arises, that arises

When this is not, that is not

This ceasing, that ceases.

The formula of Dependent Origination has twelve factors, and is primarily used to explain the process of re-birth. While the Buddha denied, on valid grounds of course, the existence of a permanent soul or ego yet he accepted the doctrine of re-birth. But the theory of re-birth in Buddhism is fundamentally different from the theory of 'transmigration of soul' in Hinduism. According to the Buddha, a being is combination of five aggregates consisting of Mind and Matter (Nama and Rupa). And the living being is conditioned—by Kamma—actions directed by the will. As long as there is this Kammic force, there is rebirth. Death is not the complete annihilation of the so-called being, for, although the organic life has ceased, the force which hitherto actuated it, is not destroyed. The Kamma force remains entirely undisturbed by the disintegration of the physical vehicle, the passing away of the present, consciousness only conditioned into conditions the coming into being of a fresh one in another birth. Each consciousness, on passing away, gives up its whole energy or all the impressions received to its successor. Each successive consciousness, therefore, consists of the potentialities of all its predecessors and something more. At death the consciousness perishes only to give birth to another in a subsequent birth.

The first link in this cycle of life, from one birth to another, is Ignorance (Avijja, Avidya) of what things truly are, and especially ignorance of the Four Noble Truths concerning the origin and cessation of suffering. Ignorance is the primary root of all evil, all moral defilements.

In brief, the formula of Dependent Origination, as enunciated by the Buddha, is as follows[8] :

"Depending on ignorance (avijja), karma-formations (sankhara) arise.

Depending on karma-formations, the consciousness that links one birth with another (vinnana) arises.

Depending on the re-linking consciousness, mind and matter (nama-rupa) arise.

Depending on mind and matter, the six sense organs (including mind) (salayatana) arise.

Depending on the six sense organs, sense-impression (phassa) arises.

Depending on the sense-impression, feeling (vedana) arises.

Depending on feelings, craving (tanha) arises.

Depending on craving, clinging (upadana) arises.

Depending on clinging, the process of becoming (bhava) arises.

Depending on the process of becoming, birth (jati) arises.

Depending on birth, arise old age, death, grief, lamentation, pain, depression and despair (jara-marana)."

In reverse order, the Dependent Origination is as follows[9] :

"With the complete and final cessation of ignorance, the karma formations do not arise.

With the cessation of the re-linking consciousness, mind and matter do not arise.

With the cessation of the mind and matter, the six sense-organs do not arise.

With the cessation of the six sense-organs, sense-impression does not arise.

With the cessation of sense-impression, feelings do not arise.

With the cessation of feelings, craving does not arise.

With the cessation of craving, clinging does not arise.

With the cessation of clinging, becoming does not arise.

With the cessation of becoming, birth does not arise.

With the cessation of birth, old age, death, sorrow, lamentation, pain, depression and despair do not arise.

Thus the entire mass of suffering ceases."

In other words, 'If we put an end to ignorance, then there will be no blind reactions that bring in their wake all manner of suffering. And if there is no more suffering, then we shall experience real peace, real happiness. The wheel of suffering can change into the wheel of liberation.'

7. THE DOCTRINE OF AHIMSA

The doctrine of Ahimsa or Non-killing is one of the fundamental teachings of the Buddha. The Five Moral Precepts (Pancha Sila) are the essential minimum to be observed by any votary of Buddhism. And significantly enough, Ahimsa or non-killing is the very first precept, viz. Panatipata veramani sikkhapadam samadiyami—I undertake the precept to abstain from the taking of life. Hence, the Buddhist should neither destroy, nor cause, nor allow to be destroyed, any living thing. In the Sutta Nipata, the Buddha clearly says[10] :

"Do not kill a living being. You should not kill or condone killing by others. Having abandoned the use of violence, you should not use force against either the strong or the feeble."

The Prakrit Dhammapada says[11] :

"He who for a hundred years makes a thousand sacrifices each month is not worth the sixteenth part of a person who is compassionate to (any) living creature."

The Blessed One's Ahimsa flows from His boundless compassion. In fact, the Buddha was, of all the religious teachers, the most compassionate. He is called the

Compassionate One, the Mahakarunika. The Buddha says[12] :

"All tremble before violence; to all life is dear. Comparing others with oneself, one should not slay or cause to slay."

And again He says[13] :

"A man is not noble in that he does harm to living beings. He who is harmless to all living beings, that one is called "noble".

The Buddha says further:

"Let him not destroy, or cause to be destroyed, any life at all or sanction the acts of those who do so. Let him refrain even from hurting any creature, both those that are strong, and those that tremble in the world."

In the Karaniya Metta Sutta, the Blessed One says[14]:

"Let no one deceive or despise another person anywhere; let no one wish harm to another out of anger or ill-will. Just as a mother protects her only child with her own life, so should there be developed in all living beings a mind without limit. And in all the world let there be developed a mind of loving kindness without limit, above, below, across, without obstruction, without enmity, without rivalry."

Prior to the advent of the Buddha, the cult of sacrifices had a powerful hold on the minds of the early Aryans. Not only the slaughter of animals formed part of these sacrifices but the slaughtered animal was often intended for food. In fact, the Aryans ate beef, and termed a guest 'goghana' 'one for whom a cow is slain'. The Buddha condemned the bloody sacrifices and exhorted the people to abjure violence, to show compassion towards all living beings. The Buddhist appeal to humanity was so strong that by and by the Indians turned to vegetarian diet.

The doctrine of Ahimsa preached by the Buddha was objected to by some persons, saying, that it involved surrender or non-resistance to evil. And some detractors of the Buddha even say that as a result of the Ahimsa preached by Him, India became weak. But such a view is complete mis-representation of the Buddhist doctrine of Ahimsa. No doubt, the Buddha denounced Himsa (violence) and advocated ban on killing of animals for the sake of food, sacrifice, sport or pleasure but it is wrong to interpret that He banned Himsa under all circumstances. The doctrine of Ahimsa taught by Him was fundamental, and not absolute. He stood for Ahimsa. He denounced Himsa. But He did not deny that Himsa may be the last resort to save good being destroyed by evil. It is noteworthy that for a prospecting Bhikkhu, the Blessed One has prescribed, inter-alia, the condition that he should not have run away from the Army. This means that the Buddha attached great importance to the country, and did not like the soldiers joining the Bhikkhu Sangha in order to avoid fighting. He differentiated between the principle of 'need to kill' and 'will to kill'. While He taught that there should be 'no will to kill' yet He did not rule out the possibility of 'need to kill' under desperate circumstances.

Once the Buddha was questioned on the subject

of Ahimsa by Siha, a General in the army of the Licchavis of Vaisali, and a follower of Mahavira. After he had embraced Buddhism, General Siha asked the Buddha:

"I am a soldier, O Blessed One, and am appointed by the king to enforce his laws and to wage his wars. Does the Tathagata, who teaches kindness without end and compassion with all sufferers, permit the punishment of the criminal? And further, does the Tathagata declare that it is wrong to go to war for the protection of our homes, our wives, our children and our property. Does the Tathagata maintain that all strifes, including such warfare as is waged for a righteous cause, should be forbidden ?"

The Lord replied:

"He who deserves punishment must be punished, and he who is worthy of favour must be favoured. Yet at the same time. Tathagata teaches to do no injury to any living being but to be full of love and kindness. These injunctions are not contradictory, for whosoever must be punished for the crimes which he has committed suffers his injury not through the ill-will of the judge but on account of his evil-doing. His own acts have brought upon him the injury that the executor of the law inflicts".

Doubtless, the Buddha taught that evil should be cured by the return of good. But He never preached that evil should be allowed to overpower good. Hence, if driven to the wall, a Buddhist can fight in self-defence and he must fight.

8. THE FOLLY OF CASTE

Prior to the advent of the Buddha, India was unaware of the ethics of equality and universal brotherhood. According to the Purusha Sukta of the Rig Veda, the Brahmins came from the mouth, Kshatriyas from the arms, Vaishyas from the thighs, and Shudras from the feet of the Brahma, the Creator. This society based on the mythical origin was known as Chaturvana and was regulated by the principle of graded inequality; the Brahmins being at the top, followed by Kshatriyas, Vaishyas and Shudras in descending order. This rule of graded inequality regulated their rights and privileges as well. Even the punishments for secular offences were based on the principle of inequality; the Brahmins always getting the minimum and the Shudras maximum punishments.

The Buddha revolted against such oppressive social laws and condemned the caste system. He challenged the divine origin of the caste, and showed the hollowness of the claim of the Brahmins of having been born from the mouth of Brahma. He also refuted the Brahmin claim that only they could attain spiritual virtues, and asserted that a man of any caste, colour or creed can develop in his heart such virtues. He further said: "Let no person, whether man or woman, whatever be his or her socio-economic background, be hindred from reaching the highest perfection, which is every one's right, and within every-one's reach, and more than that, is achievable by the dint of one's own ceaseless striving."

The Enlightened One further pointed that all human beings were alike and to divide them artificially was a folly. He said that in the case of animal life there are different varieties based on different essential characteristics. So is the case with the plant life. But there do not exist such differences which justify classification of human beings into water-tight compartments as all human beings are one and the same in their essential characteristics. By birth and descent all men are alike. Therefore the Buddha asserted in a forceful manner that 'worth', based on deeds, rather that 'birth', an accidental thing, should be the measure of man. The Buddha also took concrete steps to eradicate the evil of caste. These steps were: exposing the myth of hereditary superiority claimed by the Brahmins; encouraging the down-trodden by dining at their houses; and accepting the low and lowly as equal members of the Sangha. Exhorting the Bhikkhus to forget their caste labels, the Buddha once said: "Just O brethren, as the great rivers—Ganga, Yamuna, Aciravati, Saraswati and Mahi —when they have fallen into the great ocean, lose their different names and are known as the great ocean—just so, O brethren, do these four castes—Kshatriya, Brahmins, Vaishyas and Shudras—when they begin to follow the doctrine and discipline as propounded by the Tathagata, they renounce different names of castes and ranks and become members of one and the same society."

The philosophy of liberty, equality and fraternity enunciated by the Buddha was a great boon to the oppressed society, and was whole-heartedly welcomed by the Kshatriyas, Vaishyas and Shudras. But the emphasis on 'equality' by the Buddha was an eye-sore to the Brahmins. They were not willing to take it lying down, and challenged the Buddha on this issue. Once they sent one of their clever man, Assalayana, to the

Buddha to controvert His views against caste and inequality. Assalayana went to the Buddha and pleaded his case in favour of the superiority of the Brahmins. He said[15] :

"Good Gotama, brahmans say: Just brahmans form the best caste, other castes are low; only the brahman is a fair caste, other castes are dark; only brahmans are pure, not non-brahmans; only brahmans are own sons of Brahma, born of his mouth, born of Brahma, formed by Brahma, heirs of Brahma. What do you say ?"

"But Assalayana, brahman women have their periods, conceive, give birth, and give suck. And yet these brahmans, born of women like everyone else, say that only brahmans form the best caste, and so on."

The Buddha's answer as to why the Brahmin is brought forth from the womb of a woman in exactly the same way as a person of any other caste, simply put the Assalayana on the mat. He had no answer. The Buddha then asked another question:

"Have you heard that in some of the adjacent countries there are only two castes—masters and slaves, and that (a member of) the master (caste) can become a (member of) the slave (caste), and vice versa?

"Yes, I have heard so," replied Assalayana.

"If your Chaturvana is an ideal society, why is it not universal ?"

Assalayana had no answer.

The Buddha asked further:

"Now, what do you think, Assalayana ? Is it only a brahman who, in this district, can develop a heart of love that is peaceable and kindly—not a noble, not a merchant, not a worker ?"

"No, good Gotama, (Members of) all four castes are able to do this".

What do you think, Assalayana ? Is it only a brahman who taking a string of bath-balls and powder, having gone to a river, is able to cleanse himself of dust and mud—not a noble, not a merchant, not a worker ?"

"No, good Gotama (Members of) all four castes are able to do this."

The Buddha further asked: "Does fire show any special regard to differences of caste ? Does not the fire obtained by the members of the so-called high caste by rubbing costly fragrant sticks arise just in the same way as when the members of the so-called lowest caste rub pieces of wood from sticks of an ordinary shrub—would this fire have neither flame no hue nor brilliance so that it would not be possible for it to serve the purpose of a fire ?"

"No, good Gotama. It is possible to make all the fires, in regard to flame, hue, and brilliance, serve the purpose of a fire, no matter the member of whatever family it was who lit them and no matter whatever was the kind of wood he used."

So Assalayana, "I say that all the four castes are equal; all the four castes are pure."

As Assalayana was unable to defend the Brahminic theory of caste and inequality, he threw up hands in disgust, and meekly asked to be accepted as a lay disciple of the Buddha.

In fine, the Buddha's message was:

A man becomes good or bad by deeds and not by birth.

9. MORAL CODE FOR THE LAITY

I. RELATIONS WITH OTHERS

Once the Buddha was staying at the Bamboo Grove near Rajagriha; and one day going out for usual morning round, He saw a strange sight. Sigala, a young householder, with wet hair, wet garments, and his clasped hands uplifted was performing the rite of worship to the six quarters of earth and sky; to the east, south, west, and north, to the nadir and the zenith. On the Buddha asking as to why he was doing so, Sigala said:

"Sir, my, father, when he was on his death-bed, said to me: 'Dear son, you should worship the quarters of earth and sky.' So, venerable sir, I am honouring the words of my father."

"But, young householder, this is not the way to worship the six quarters."

"How then, sir, the six quarters should be worshipped", asked Sigala.

Then the Blessed One said[16] that the following should be looked upon as the six quarters; parents as the east; teachers as the south; wife and children as the west; friends and companions as the north; servants and the employees as the nadir; men devoted to the religious life as the zenith. Then, the Buddha described the chief duties men owe to one another under the following six heads:

(i) Parents and Children

Parents should:

1. Restrain their children from vice.
2. Train them in virtue.
3. Have them taught arts or sciences.
4. Provide them with suitable wives or husbands.
5. Give them their inheritance.

The Child should:

1. Support them who supported him.
2. Perform family duties incumbent on him.
3. Guard their property.
4. Make himself worthy to be their heir.
5. Honour their memory, when they are gone.

(ii) Pupils and Teachers

The pupil should honour his teachers:

1. By rising in their presence.
2. By ministering to them.
3. By obeying them.
4. By supplying their wants.
5. By attention to instruction.

The teacher should show his affection to his pupils:

1. By training them in all that is good.
2. By teaching them to hold knowledge fast.
3. By instruction in science and lore.
4. By speaking well of them to their friends and companions.
5. By guarding them from danger.

(iii) Husband and Wife

The husband should cherish his wife:

1. By treating her with respect.
2. By treating her with kindness.
3. By being faithful to her.
4. By causing her to be honoured by others.
5. By giving her suitable ornaments and clothes.

The wife should show her affection for her husband:

1. By ordering her household aright.
2. By being hospitable to kinsmen and friends.
3. By being a chaste wife.
4. By being a thrifty housekeeper.
5. By showing skill and diligence in all she has to do.

(iv) Friends and Companions

The honourable man should minister to his friends:

1. By giving presents.
2. By courteous speech.
3. By promoting their interest.
4. By treating them as his equals.
5. By sharing with them his prosperity.

They should show their attachment to him:

1. By watching over him when he is off his guard.
2. By guarding his property when he is careless.
3. By offering him a refuge in danger.
4. By adhering to him in misfortune.
5. By showing kindness to his family.

(v) Masters and Servants

The master should provide for the welfare of his servants:

1. By apportioning work to them according to their strength.
2. By supplying suitable food and wages.
3. By tending them in sickness.
4. By sharing with them unusual delicacies.
5. By now and then granting them holidays.

They should show their attachment to him as follows:

1. By rising before him.
2. By retiring later to rest.
3. By being content with what is given them.
4. By working cheerfully and thoroughly.
5. By speaking well of him (and also properly to him).

(vi) Duty towards Religious Teachers

The householder should minister to religious teachers:

1. By affection in act.
2. By affection in words.
3. By affection in thoughts.
4. By giving them a ready welcome.
5. By supplying their temporal wants.

They should show their affection to him:

1. By dissuading him from vice.
2. By exhorting him to virtue.

3. By feeling kindly towards him.
4. By instructing him in religion.
5. By clearing up his doubts, and by pointing the way to liberation.

II. THE CODE FOR WOMEN

1. There are four different types of women[17] :

First, there are those who become angry for slight causes, who have changeable minds, who are greedy, jealous of other's happiness, and who have no sympathy for the needs of the others.

Second, there are those who grow angry over ordinary affairs, who are fickle and greedy, but who do not envy others their happiness and who are sympathetic for the needs of others.

Third, there are those who are more broad-minded and who do not become angry very often, and who know to control a greedy mind, but who are not able to avoid feelings of jealousy and who are not sympathetic.

Fourth, there are those who are broad-minded, who can restrain feelings of greed and retain a calm mind, who do not envy other their happiness, and who are sympathetic for the needs of others.

2. When a young woman marries she should make the following resolutions[18] :

"I must honour the parents of my husband. They have given us all the advantages we have and our wise protectors, so I must serve them with appreciation and be ready to help them whenever I can.

"I must be respectful to my husband's teacher because he has given my husband a sacred teaching and we could not live as human beings without the guidance of the sacred teachings.

"I must cultivate my mind so that I will be able to understand my husband and be able to help in his work. I must never be indifferent to my husband's interest, thinking they are his affairs and not mine.

"I must study the nature, ability and tastes of the family and of the servants so that I can conserve the income of my husband and not waste it."

3. The young wife of the eldest son of the rich merchant, Anathapindika, was proud and arrogant and did not listen to the instruction of her husband and his parents and consequently there was trouble in the family. One day the Blessed One came to visit Anathapindika and noticed it. He called her to him and spoke to her kindly saying,[19] "There are seven types of wives:

First, a wife who is like a murderer. She has an impure mind, does not honour her husband and then loses her heart to another man.

Second, a wife who is like a thief. She never considers for her husband's labour but thinks only of her desire for luxury. She wastes her husband's income to satisfy her appetite and by so doing steals from him.

Third, a wife is like a master. She rails at her husband, neglects the house-keeping and thinks only of her own comfort.

Fourth, a wife who is like a mother. She cares for her husband as though he were a child, she protects her husband as a mother does her son, and she looks after his income as though he was incapable of doing so.

Fifth, a wife who is like a sister. She is faithful to her husband and serves him like a sister with modesty and reserve.

Sixth, a wife who is like a friend. She tries to please her husband like a friend who has just returned from a long absence. She is modest, behaves nicely and treats her husband with great respect.

Seventh, a wife who is like a maid-servant. She serves her husband well and with fidelity. She respects him, obeys his commands, has no wishes of her own, no ill-feeling, no resentment, and always tries to make him happy."

The Buddha asked her, "Sujata, which type of wife you are or would you like to be ?"

Hearing the kind words of the Blessed One, she was ashamed of her past conduct and replied that she would like to be a wife like a maid-servant. She changed her life and became her husband's helper and together they sought enlightenment.

III. LIFE'S HIGHEST BLESSINGS

What are the Life's Highest Blessings ? This significant question was once posed to the Buddha while He was staying at Sravasti, in Jeta grove, in Anathapindika's monastery. The questioner reverently asked the Buddha:

"Many gods and men, longing for happiness, have pondered on Blessings, tell thou (me) the Highest Blessing."

The Blessed One declared[20] as many as 38 Highest Blessings in the following manner:

"Not to associate with fools, to associate with the wise and to honour those who are worthy of honour—this is the Highest Blessing. (1-3)

To live in a suitable place, to have done meritorious deeds in the past, and to set oneself in the right direction—this is the Highest Blessing. (4-6)

Ample learning, skill in crafts, a well-learnt discipline, pleasant speech and peaceful occupation, this is the Highest Blessing. (7-10).

Supporting one's father and mother, protecting wife and children, and peaceful occupation—this is the Highest Blessing. (11-13)

Liberality, righteous living, the helping of relatives, and blameless actions—this is the Highest Blessing. (14-17)

To cease and abstain from evil, to refrain from intoxicating drinks, and diligence in the Dhamma—this is the Highest Blessing. (18-21)

Reverence, humility, contentment, gratitude, the timely hearing of the Dhamma—this is the Highest Blessing. (22-26)

Patience, obedience, seeing the monks (holy men), and discussing the Dhamma at proper times—this is the Highest Blessing (27-30).

Self-control, holy life, insight into the Four Noble Truths, and the realization of Nibbana—this is the Highest Blessing. (31-34)

If a man's mind is sorrowless, stainless, secure, and is not shaken when touched by the things of the world—this is the Highest Blessing. (35-38)

Those who, thus acting, are undefeated in every respect attain happiness everywhere—to them these are the Highest Blessings."

10. GEMS FROM THE DHAMMAPADA

Buddhism is, in essence, a way of life. And Dhammapada, the well-known anthology of 423 select sayings of the Buddha is the best guide for any one willing to follow the Buddhist way of life. "One never turns in vain", says an admirer, "to these stanzas of incomparable beauty for advice, for alleviation of life's manifold pains, or for message of cheer and penetrating insight". Here is a selection of 101 Gems from the Dhammapada to,* the most famous Buddhist scripture.

I. YAMAKAVAGGA. THE PAIRS

1. All mental states have mind as their forerunner, mind is their chief, and they are mind-made. If, with an impure mind, one speaks or acts then suffering follows one even as the wheel, the hoof of the ox (who is drawing a cart). (1).
2. Mind is the forerunner of all mental states; mind is their chief, and they are mind-made. If with a pure mind, one speaks or acts, happiness follows

---

* As translated by Ven. A.P. Buddhadatta Maha Thera.

him close like his never-departing shadow. (2)

3. Hatred never ceases by hatred in this world. Through loving-kindness it comes to an end. This is an ancient Law. (5)
4. Whosoever lives delighting in visual forms with senses unsubdued, immoderate in food, sluggish and inert,-him verily does Mara over-throw as the wind a weak tree. (7).
5. Those who know the true as the true, and the false as the false, who abide in right mindedness, they arrive at the real. (12)

II. APPAMADAVAGGA. HEEDFULNESS

6. Vigilance is the way to Deathless. Negligence is the path to death. Those that are vigilant do not die. Those that are negligent are like unto the dead. (21)
7. Whosoever is energetic, mindful, pure in conduct, discriminating, self-restrained, righteous of life, vigilant,-the fame of such an one continually increases. (24)
8. By diligence, vigilance, discipline, and self-mastery, let the wise man make (for himself an) island that no flood can overcome. (25)
9. Vigilant among the negligent, wide-awake among those asleep, the wise man advances like a swift horse leaving a weak nag behind. (29)

III. CITTAVAGGA. THE MIND

10. This fickle, unsteady mind, difficult to guard, difficult to control, the wise man makes straight, as the fletcher straightens the arrow. (33)

11. Hard to control, unstable is this mind; it flits wherever it likes. Good is it to subdue the mind. A subdued mind brings happiness. (35)

12. He whose mind is inconstant, he who knows not the Good Teaching, he whose confidence wavers,—the wisdom of such a one never comes to fullness. (38)

13. Whatever harm a foe may do to a foe, or a hater to a hater,—a wrongly-directed mind may do one even greater harm. (42)

14. Neither mother, nor father, nor any other relative can do a man such good as is wrought by a rightly-directed mind. (43)

IV. PUPPHAVAGGA. THE FLOWERS

15. The man who seeks only the flowers (of sensual pleasures) whose mind is distracted,—death carries him away as a great flood a sleeping village. (47)

16. The man who seeks only the flowers (of sensual pleasures), whose mind is distracted, and who is insatiate in desires,—him the destroyer brings under his sway. (48)

17. As a beautiful flower that is brilliant of hue but yields no fragrance, even so fruitless is the well-spoken word of one who does not practise it. (51)

18. As a flower that is lovely, colourful, and fragrant, even so fruitful is the well-spoken word of one who practises it. (52.)

19. The fragrance of flowers, of sandal-wood, of tagara-plant or jasmine, is not wafted against the wind; but the fragrance of good men is wafted against the wind. The virtuous man diffuses fragrance in all directions. (54)

20. Sandal-wood, tagara-plant, water-lily, wild jasmine,-of all these kinds of fragrance, the fragrance of virtue is by far the best. (55)

21. As on a mass of refuse, thrown by the road side, springs up a sweet-smelling charming lily, so among the mass of blind worldings, who are like unto rubbish, a disciple of the fully Enlightened One outshines in wisdom. (58),(59)

V. BALAVAGGA. THE FOOL

22. Long is the night to the wakeful; long is the league to the weary; long is the circle of rebirths to fools that know not the sublime Truth. (60)

23. If a seeker should not find a companion who is better or equal, he should resolutely pursue the solitary course, there is no fellowship with the fool. (61).

24. 'I have sons, I have wealth', so thinks the fool and is troubled. Verily, he himself is not of his own. Whence sons ? Whence wealth ? (62)

25. The fool aware of his folly, in so far is wise. But the fool who thinks himself wise, is called

a fool indeed. (63).

26. Well done is that deed which, done, brings no regret; the fruit whereof is received with delight and satisfaction. (68)

27. 'It is sweet as honey', thinks the fool while as yet the evil has not ripened. But when the evil ripens, the fool comes to grief. (69)

28. Evil that is done does not immediately bear fruit as milk comes out at once (from the nipple or teat when sucked by a young one); it follows the fool like a smouldering spark that at last breaks out into flame. (71)

VI. PANDITAVAGGA. THE WISE

29. Associate not with evil companions; seek not the fellowship of the low. Consort with good companions; seek the fellowship of noble men. (78).

30. Even as a solid rock is unshaken by the wind, so do the wise remain unmoved by praise or blame. (81)

31. Few among men are they who cross to the further shore.The others, the bulk of men, run up and down the hither bank. (85)

32. They whose minds are trained to perfection in the Factors of Enlightenment, they who, without hankering, delight in the renunciation of attachment,—these, corruption free, radiant ones, have attained nibbana even in this life. (89)

VII. ARAHANTAVAGGA. THE WORTHY

33. He whose senses are mastered like horses well under their drivers' control, who is purged of pride, free from passions,—such a steadfast one even Devas hold dear. (94).

34. Tranquil is the thought, tranquil the word and deed of him who rightly knowing, is wholly freed, perfectly peaceful and equipoised. (96)

VIII. SAHASSAVAGGA. THE THOUSANDS

35. Better than a thousand verses devoid of meaning, is one verse (charged with meaning), hearing which one is pacified. (101)

36. Though one should conquer in battle thousands and thousands of men, yet he is the noblest victor who would conquer himself. (103)

37. In him who is ever inclined to honour and respect elders, these four things are increased (length of) age, beauty, happiness and strength. (109)

38. Better than a hundred years lived viciously and uncontrolled, is a single day lived virtuously and meditative. (110)

39. Better than a hundred years lived sluggishly and inactive is a single day lived strenuously and resolute. (112)

40. Better than a hundred years lived blind to the Truth Supreme, is a single day lived beholding the Truth Supreme. (115)

IX. PAPAVAGGA. EVIL

41. Make haste in doing good; check your mind from evil. Whosoever is backward in doing good, his mind delights in evil. (116)
42. If a man should do that which is good, let him do it again and again; let him turn the desires of his heart thereto. Blissful is the accumulation of good. (118)
43. Think not lightly of evil, saying: 'It will not come to me'. Even a water-pot is filled by the falling of drops. Likewise the fool, gathering little by little, fills himself with evil. (121)
44. Some are born in the womb; the evildoers are born in hell; the well-doing go to the heaven-world; the undefiled ones become extinct. (126)

X. DANDAVAGGA. PUNISHMENT

45. All tremble before punishment; all fear death. Comparing others with oneself, one should not slay, nor cause to slay. (129)
46. If you silence yourself as a gong that is broken, you have already attained nibbana; contention has no place in you. (134)
47. Neither going about naked, nor with matted locks, nor with dust on one's body, neither fasting, nor sleeping on the ground nor besmearing oneself with ashes or dirt, nor squatting on the heels, can purify a mortal who has not overcome doubts. (141)

48. Like a thorough-bred horse touched by the whip, even so be strenuous and filled with religious emotion. By confidence, virtue, effort, concentration, and investigation of the Truth, by being endowed with knowledge and conduct, and by being mindful, leave ye this great suffering behind. (144)

XI. JARAVAGGA. OLD AGE

49. Here is a city built of bones and coated with flesh and blood, wherein are deposited decay, death, pride and jealousy. (150)

50. The ignorant man lives like a bull; his bulk increases, but not his wisdom. (152).

51. They who in youth have not led the life that is best or have not gathered wealth, lie like worn out arrows, pondering over the past actions. (156)

XII. ATTAVAGGA. THE SELF

52. If one knows oneself to be dear (to oneself), let one keep close watch upon oneself. During any of the three watches the wise man should keep vigil. (157)

53. First establish thyself in the right, then thou mayest admonish others. Let not the wise man give occasion for reproach. (158)

54. One oneself is the guardian of oneself; what other guardian would there be? With oneself fully controlled, one obtains a refuge which is hard to gain. (160)

55. It is easy to do things that are bad and not beneficial to one's self. That which is good and beneficial, that is most difficult to do. (163)
56. A man defiles himself through his own evil actions; he purifies himself by avoiding evil. Purity and impurity depend on oneself. No one can purify another. (165)

XIII. LOKAVAGGA. THE WORLD

57. Do not follow mean things. Dwell not in negligence. Cherish not false views. Be not one of those that linger long in the world. (167).
58. Look upon the world as a bubble; regard the world as it were a mirage. Thus regarding the world, the Lord of Death finds thee not. (170)
59. Whosoever was negligent before, but afterwards practises vigilance, such a one illumines this world like the moon emerging from a cloud. (172)
60. Better is the fruit of Entering the Stream than sole sovereignty over the earth, than going to heaven, than rule supreme over the entire universe. (178)

XIV. BUDDHAVAGGA. THE ENLIGHTENED ONE

61. It is difficult to be born as a man; hard is the life of mortals. Difficult is to get opportunity of hearing the Sublime Truth. Difficult is the arising of Awakened Ones. (182)
62. Not to do any evil, to cultivate good, to purify

one's thoughts,—this is the Teaching of the Buddhas. (183)

63. He who seeks refuge in the Buddha, in His Teaching and His Community of monks, he who sees with right knowledge the four Noble Truths, namely, Suffering, the cause of Suffering, the transcending of Suffering and the Noble Eightfold Path which leads to the cessation of Suffering, this indeed is the refuge secure; this is the refuge supreme. Seeking such refuge one is released from all suffering. (190), (191) and (192)

64. Hard to find is the Man Supreme; such a one does not take birth everywhere. But where such a wise man is born, that family thrives happily (193).

65. He who reverences those worthy of reverence, whether the Buddhas or their disciples, who have transcended all obstacles, passed beyond the reach of distress and lamentation; he who reverences such peaceful and secure ones, — this merit cannot be measured by anyone as such and such. (195), (196)

XV. SUKHAVAGGA. HAPPINESS

66. Conquest begets enmity; the defeated lie down in distress. The peaceful lies down in happiness, giving up both victory and defeat. (201)

67. There is no fire like lust, no crime like hatred. There is no misery like the constituents of existence, no happiness higher than the Peace of Nibbana. (202)

68. Health is the highest gain; contentment is the greatest riches. A trusty friend is the best kinsman;

Nibbana is the supreme bliss. (204)

69. Good is it to behold the Noble Ones; to dwell with them is happiness. One will be ever happy by not seeing fools. (206)

70. Frequenting the company of fools, one has cause to grieve for long. Association with fools is ever painful as with a foe. To dwell together with the wise is happiness, like meeting with kinsfolk. (207)

XVI. PIYAVAGGA. AFFECTIONS

71. From attachment springs grief; from attachment springs fear. For him who is wholly free from attachment there is neither grief nor fear. (214)

72. The man who is perfect in virtue and vision, is righteous, and has realised the Truths, who fulfils that which he himself ought to do,—him do people hold dear. (217)

XVII. KODHAVAGGA. ANGER

73. One should give up anger, renounce pride, and overcome all fetters. Whosoever clings not to the constituents of existence, and to nothing whatsoever,—sufferings never befall him. (221)

74. Overcome anger by loving-kindness, evil by good. Conquer the niggardly with liberality, with truth the speaker of falsehoods. (223)

75. Speak the truth; give not way to anger, give of your little to him that asks of you; by these three things one may go to the realm of gods. (224)

XVIII. MALAVAGGA. IMPURITIES

76. Make an island or refuge for yourself; strive hard and be wise. Free from defilement, cleansed of stain, you shall not come again to birth and decay. (238)

77. By degrees, little by little, from time to time, a wise man should remove his own impurities, as a smith removes the dross of silver.(239)

78. Whosoever in this world destroys life, utters lies, takes what is not given, goes after the wives of others, is addicted to intoxicating drinks, such a one digs up his own roots in this very world, (246), (247)

79. There is no fire like lust. There is no grip like anger. There is no net like delusion. There is no river like craving. (251)

80. Easy to perceive is the fault of others; one's own, however, is hard to perceive. Like chalf one winnows other's faults; but one's own one conceals as the cheating gambler an unlucky throw. (252)

XIX. DHAMMATTAVAGGA. THE RIGHTEOUS

81. A man is not righteous because he arbitrates hastily. A wise man who investigates both right and wrong, who judges others with due deliberation, with judgement righteous and just, that wise one, guarded of the Teaching, is called 'righteous'. (256), (257)

82. He is not versed in the Dhamma merely because he speaks much. He who hears little

(of the Teachings), but sees the Truth mentally, and observes it well in deed, he is called 'versed in the Dhamma'. (259)

83. In whom are truth, virtue, harmlessness and self-mastery, who is free from defilement, and wise,—he truly is called an Elder. (261)

84. A man is not noble in that he works harm to living creatures. Whosoever is harmless towards all living beings,—he is called noble. (270)

XX. MAGGAVAGGA. THE PATH

85. Best of paths is the Eightfold Path; best of truths are the Four (Noble Truths). Best of conditions is Passionlessness; best of bipeds is the Seeing One, (the Man of Vision). (273)

86. You yourselves should make an effort; the Awakened Ones are only teachers. The devoted to meditation arrive at release from the bonds of Mara. (276)

87. 'All compounded things are transient; when one sees this with wisdom, then one becomes disgusted of the painful. This is the Path to Purity. (277)

XXI. PAKINNAKAVAGGA. MISCELLANEOUS

88. If by renouncing a lesser happiness, one may behold a greater happiness, let the wise man, forsake the lesser, having regard to the greater. (290)

89. He who is full of faith and virtue, possessed

of repute and wealth, in whatever land he travels, he is respected everywhere. (303)

XXII. NIRAYAVAGGA. WOEFUL STATE

90. Four misfortunes befall a heedless man who commits adultery: demerit, uneasy slumbers, ill repute as the third, and purgatory as the fourth. (309)

91. Those who think there is evil where there is none, and do not see evil where evil is, such beings embracing false views go to the woeful state. (318)

XXIII. NAGAVAGGA. THE ELEPHANT

92. If you get a prudent companion who is fit to live with you, who behaves well, and is wise, you should live with him joyfully and mindfully overcoming all dangers. (328)

93. It is better to live alone; with the foolish there is no fellowship. Living alone one avoids evil, and is free from care like an elephant that wanders through the forest. (330)

94. Good is a friend in need. Good is contentment with whatever betides. Good is a store of merit at the end of life. Good is it to leave all sorrow behind. (331)

95. Good is it to honour mother; good is it to honour father. Good is it to honour ascetics, and good is it to honour the Noble Ones. (332)

96. Good is practice of virtue one's whole lifelong. Good is confidence that stands firm. Good is

the acquisition of wisdom. Good is abstinence from evil. (333)

XXIV. TANHAVAGGA. CRAVING

97. Be free from the past, be free from the future, be free from the present. Crossing to the farther shore of existence, with mind released everywhere, no more shalt thou come to birth and decay. (348)

98. He who delights in subduing thoughts, who meditates on impurities, and is ever mindful,— it is he who will make an end of craving; he will cut Mara's bond. (350)

99. The gift of Dhamma excells all gifts. The flavour of Dhamma excells all flavours. The delight in Dhamma excells all delights. Victory over all suffering is the ending of craving. (354)

XXV. BHIKKHUVAGGA. THE MENDICANT

100. Good is restraint of sight. Good is restraint of hearing. Good is restraint of smell. Good is restraint of taste. (360)

101. Oneself is one's own protector; oneself is one's own refuge. Control, therefore, your own self as a merchant, control's a spirited charger. (380)

REFERENCES

2. What is Nirvana?
   1. The Fire Sermon, Samyutta Nikaya, 35,28.
   2. Samyutta Nikaya, III,189.
   3. Anguttara Nikaya, III,55.

3. The Path to Nirvana
   4. Vinaya Mahavagga-I, Dhamma-cakkappavattana Sutta.
   5. Anguttara Nikaya, IV, 67-68.

4. The Law of Karma
   6. Digha Nikaya, 13, Tevijja Sutta.

5. No-Soul Doctrine.
   7. Vinaya I, 13-14, Anatta-lakkhana Sutta.

6. Dependent Origination
   8. Samyutta Nikaya, XII,1.
   9. Ibid.

7. The Doctrine of Ahimsa
   10. Sutta Nipata, Dhammika Sutta.
   11. The Prakarit Dhammapada, Sahasavagga 16.
   12. Dhammapada, 130.
   13. Dhammapada, 270
   14. Sutta Nipata, Metta Sutta.

8. The Folly of Caste.
   15. Majjhima Nikaya, 93, Assalayana Sutta.

9. Moral Code for the Laity.
   16. Digha Nikaya, Sigalavada Sutta.
   17. Anguttara Nikaya, IV, 197.
   18. Anguttara Nikaya, V, 333, Uggaha Sutta.
   19. Anguttara Nikaya, VII, 59, Sujata Sutta.
   20. Khuddaka Patha, Mangala Sutta.

8

THE SANGHA: HOLY ORDER

The Sangha, the Holy Order, of both monks and nuns, is the unique monastic organisation founded by the Buddha. Those who renounce the life of a householder and take to the life of a recluse by joining the Sangha are known as Bhikkhus or monks. The word Bhikkhu or Bhikshu means mendicant, a monk living on alms. A Bhikkhu is not a priest in the sense of theistic religions. He is not only committed to his own spiritual development and attainment of Nirvana, the highest bliss, but also to help others in their efforts at spiritual progress. A Bhikkhu while striving for his own salvation also acts as a friend, philosopher and guide of the laity in all religious and spiritual matters. Hence, a Bhikkhu is the torch-bearer of the Dhamma.

When the Buddha founded the Bhikkhu Sangha and asked His first sixty disciples to go out and wander forth for the gain of the many, for the welfare of the many, He had no set plans for the Organisation as such. A Bhikkhu was required to take five vows, that is, to remain celebate, not to commit theft, not to tell lies, not to kill or take life, and not to own anything except the following eight articles: the three pieces of cloth to cover his body, two under-garments and one loose robe to cover the whole of the body, except the right shoulder; a girdle for the loins; an alms-bowl; a razor; a needle; and a water strainer. The monks were also required to take solid food only once a day, and that too before noon.

When, however, the Dhamma spread and the number of those seeking the way to Nirvana increased, the need arose of some norms for regulating the life pattern and behaviour of those joining the Sangha. In due course, an eleborate code of conduct for the Bhikkhus and Bhikkhunies was farmulated by the Buddha. In the Pali Vinaya Pitaka, the number of Vinaya rules is 227 for the monks, and 311 for the nuns.

In the Vinaya for the Bhikkhus there are four rules the transgression of which makes a monk liable to permanent expulsion from the Sangha. There are 13 rules in the Sangadhisesa. If any of these rules are transgressed, the monk concerned should spend a period of expiation away from the Sangha and obtain clearance from the Sangha by applying for abbhana-karma. The Nissaggiya Pacittiya contains 30 rules. These rules concern wrong use of certain articles by Sangha. A monk who violates any of these rules should vest in the Sangha the article concerned (such as an alsm-bowl or a robe) and obtain purification by making a formal confession. There are 92 rules known as "Pactiya". Breach of these rules compels the Bhikkhu to go before a confessor and confess his guilt. He should have sincere intentions on such occasions and get himself repurified, promising never to repeat the guilt again. There are also 75 rules dealing with such modes of behaviour connected with wearing of robes, preaching the doctrine, taking meals, going for alms in villages. This ethical code is known as "Sekhiya". The transgressor of these rules could confess his guilt before another monk and get himself purified.

Primarily, the Vinaya deals with the self-development of the monks, and the way of life in the monasteries. But a good number of these rules are directly concerned with the laity-upasakas and upasikas also. While supporting the Sangha, the laity also kept a watch on their conduct and made critical comments as and when they found the conduct of the Bhikkhus and Bhikkhunies wanting. No wonder, many a rules were laid down by the Master when certain lapses by the Bhikkhus were brought to His notice by the people. We often find such instances where the people murmured, were annoyed, and became indignant, saying, 'How can the Sakyaputtiya Bhikkhus do such and such thing? The Bhikkhus heard the people so murmuring and told the matter to the Blessed One. Then He laid down the rule. This shows the Buddha was quite responsive to the wishes of the laity.

The Buddha also introduced the observance of the fortnightly self-purificatory meeting, called Uposatha. In these fortnightly meetings, the Vinaya rules, the Patimokkha, were recited, and the monks and nuns assembled there were required to confess any act or omission or commission during the preceding fortnight. The deliberations in these meetings and other meetings of the Sangha were conducted in a democratic manner. In the Buddhist Sangha, the 'Speaker' was called 'Asanaprajanpaka'. The motion (Jnapti) was put before the House thrice. If all remained silent, it was considered as passed unanimously. In the case of a difference of opinion, the matter was settled by 'Yebhuyyasika' i.e. by the vote of the majority. The voting ticket or ballot was called 'Salaka.' The officials who collected Salakas were called "Salaka-gahapakas." Thus the regulation of the debate in the Sangha was of a highly developed order and was truly democratic.

Another significant practice introduced by the Buddha was the observance of the Vassa, the Retreat during the three months of the rainy season by the monks and nuns. During this period, the monks and nuns remained stationary and did not tour from place to place. The Vassa period acted as a great combining force in the Buddhist organisation as it brought together the monks and laity to the mutual advantage of both.

The Sangha was well-established during the life time of the Buddha and there were a number of enlightened monks spreading the glorious doctrine of the Blessed One. When the Master had gone, the Bhikkhu Sangha took steps to codify and preserve the Teachings of the Buddha. For this purpose, a Council or Sangiti was held at Rajagaha, modern Rajgir in Bihar, in which five hundred Arhats, the holiest of the holy, participated. After a great deal of scrutiny, the venerable monks led by Maha Kassapa, Ananda and Upali, settled the full text of the Buddha-Word, the Pali Tripitaka. Ever since then, the Sangha has played a very crucial role in the preservation and propagation of the Dhamma.

APPENDIX

BUDDHISM IN MODERN INDIA

For about 200 years after the Maha-parinirvana of the Buddha in BC 483, Buddhism was in the making and being developed. Then came Asoka (BC-273-232), the third Mauryan Emperor, who after finding solace in the Buddha-Dhamma, launched a vigorous campaign to preach and propagate the message of the Buddha. With his systematic and energetic efforts, Asoka took out Buddhism from the monasteries and made it a national religion. Thereafter, Buddhism dominated the Indian scene for 1000 years. Besides the powerful kings like Kanishka, Harsha and other royal houses, this period saw the emergence of a galaxy of Buddhist saints and scholars who made immense contribution to the Buddhist philosophy and religion. Not only that, the religion of the Buddha was always the first choice of the thinkers and philosophers of ancient India. The princes, nobles and elite always considered it their honour to associate themselves one way or the other with the great name of the Buddha. The depressed and oppressed masses too found solace and inspiration in Teachings of the Buddha.

The religion of the Buddha began declining in India from the eighth century onward, and by the twelfth century it was confined to a small pocket in Bihar and Bengal. Thereafter, Buddhism completely disappeared from the land of its birth. The reasons for its decline and disappearance from India were many and varied into which we need not go here. The Dark Age of Buddhism in India from 1200 to 1800 A.D. was in fact the darkest. During this period, thousands of Viharas, Stupas and Monasteries were destroyed and plundered by the opponents of Buddhism on the one hand, and completely ignored and allowed to decay by the Buddhists on the other hand. A good number of the Buddhist temples were also converted into Hindu and Muslim places of worship. These included the Maha Bodhi Temple at Bodh Gaya as well which was occupied by a Hindu Mahant some time in the sixteenth century. Thus, by and by every trace of Buddhism was effaced from the land of its birth.

The Buddhist revival movement in India began in 1891 with the arrival of Anagarika Dharmpala, a great son of Sri Lanka. The Maha Bodhi Society of India founded by him, and other pioneers were able to create a lot of awareness about the rich heritage of Buddhism but they were not able to attract many adherents to its fold. Then came Dr. Ambedkar who performed a mircale at Nagpur on 14 October, 1956 by bringing about half a million people to the refuge of the Buddha. Though, Dr.Ambedkar passed away within two months of this historic event but the conversions continued unabated.

Buddhism in India has come a long way since the

revival movement began a hundred years ago. As against a meagre population of about 50,000 in 1891, India now has over five million Buddhists constituting 0.71 per cent of the total population of the country. In modern India, majority of the Buddhists follow the Theravada tradition. The Buddhists living in the high Himalayan valleys are Mahayanists. The Indian Buddhists can be further divided into four distinct groups. Firstly, there are survivals from the Buddhist period. Secondly, there are the ethnic over-laps from the neighbouring countries, such as Nepal, Thailand and Burma. The third category is represented by those who were attracted towards Buddhism as a result of the missionary movement spearheaded by the Maha Bodhi Society. The followers of Dr. B.R. Ambedkar, who adopted the Buddhist way of life in October 1956 and after, form the fourth group. The Tibetans, who migrated to India in the wake of the flight of His Holiness the Dalai Lama from Tibet to India in 1959, form yet another group. Of all the groups, the followers of Dr. Ambedkar form the most dominant group. They are as many as 90 per cent of the total Buddhist population in India. And out of them, 84 per cent live in Maharashtra, the home state of Dr. Babasaheb Ambedkar.

There are a number of Buddhist sites and shrines in modern India. Of these, sixteen are more important. Firstly, there are the four sacred shrines associated directly with the four principal events in the life of the Buddha. These are:

1. Lumbini (In Nepal), the birth place of the Buddha.

2. Bodh Gaya (Bihar), where the Buddha attained Enlightenment.
3. Sarnath (near Varanasi, Uttar Pradesh), where the Buddha preached His First Sermon.
4. Kushinagar (Uttar Pradesh), where the Buddha attained Maha-parinirvana.

To these be added, four other places which were also sancitfied by the Buddha. These are:

1. (Rajgir) (Rajagaha), in Bihar, where the Buddha spent several years, and where the first Buddhist Council met after the Maha-parinir-vana of the Buddha.
2. Vaisali (Bihar), which the Buddha visited on numerous occasions, and where the second Buddhist Council was held after about hundred years of the demise of the Buddha.
3. Sravasti (Uttar Pradesh), where the Buddha spent twenty-five Vassa (annual rains) retreats in the Jetavana Vihara donated by Anathapindika.
4. Sankissa (Uttar Pradesh), where the Buddha is said to have descended from Tusita Heaven after preaching to His mother.

Besides these eight sacred shrines there are eight more Buddhist sites and shrines in modern India. These are :

1. Nalanda (Bihar), the site of the world famous Buddhist University.
2. Sanchi (Madhya Pradesh), the site of the most

ancient and magnificent Stupas from which the relics of Sariputta, Mahamoggallana, Moggaliputta Tissa and nine other Buddhist saints were discovered.

3. Amaravati (Andhra Pradesh), the most ancient Buddhist monument known for its art and architecture.
4. Nagarjunakonda (Andhra Pradesh), where the famous saint and scholar, the founder of the Madhymika school, Nagarjuna lived in the second century A.D.
5. The four well-known Buddhist Cave Temples—Ajanta, Ellora, Kanheri and Karla—all in Maharashtra.

In brief, Buddhism in India has regained much of its lost prestige. The Buddhist sacred shrines have since been repaired and renovated to a great extent, and are once again humming with the sweet sound of 'Buddham Saranam Gacchami'. Also, the Blessed One is now the guiding star of a vast multitude in India. And to cater to the spiritual and religious needs of the ever-increasing Buddhist population, a large number of Viharas have come up, and the number of Bhikkhus has increased. The most sacred and the most important festival of the Buddhists, known as Buddha Purnima or Buddha Jayanti is now a National Holiday in India. Not only that, the Buddhist symbols have also been adopted as National Symbols. The capital of Asoka's

Pillar at Sarnath has been adopted as the National Emblem by modern India. And the Buddhist Wheel of Law (Dharma Chakra) adorns the central part of the National Flag of India. Verily, Buddhism is once again a living spiritual force in India.

INDEX